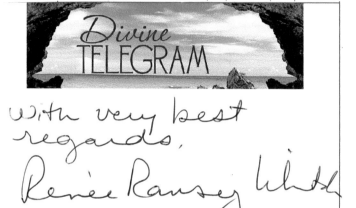

with very best
regards,

Renée Ramsey Whitehk

www.divinetelegram.com

Divine
Telegram

Renee Ramsey Whitaker

BALBOA
PRESS
A DIVISION OF HAY HOUSE

Balboa Press books may be ordered through booksellers or by contacting:

Balboa Press
A Division of Hay House
1663 Liberty Drive
Bloomington, IN 47403
www.balboapress.com
1 (877) 407-4847

Because of the dynamic nature of the Internet, any web addresses or links contained in this book may have changed since publication and may no longer be valid. The views expressed in this work are solely those of the author and do not necessarily reflect the views of the publisher, and the publisher hereby disclaims any responsibility for them.

The author of this book does not dispense medical advice or prescribe the use of any technique as a form of treatment for physical, emotional, or medical problems without the advice of a physician, either directly or indirectly. The intent of the author is only to offer information of a general nature to help you in your quest for emotional and spiritual well-being. In the event you use any of the information in this book for yourself, which is your constitutional right, the author and the publisher assume no responsibility for your actions.

Any people depicted in stock imagery provided by Thinkstock are models, and such images are being used for illustrative purposes only.
Certain stock imagery © Thinkstock.

Printed in the United States of America.

ISBN: 978-1-4525-9224-4 (sc)
ISBN: 978-1-4525-9222-0 (hc)
ISBN: 978-1-4525-9223-7 (e)

Library of Congress Control Number: 2014902379

Balboa Press rev. date: 02/13/2014

Contents

Divine Telegram is dedicated to my precious family. Each of them is an essential part of my life and I treasure them. I thank Don Whitaker, Paige Piper, Jeremy Piper, Brooke Schmidly, Derrick Caudill, Cole Ramsey Piper, and Sierra Caudill. Each of them offers something unique and indispensable. Together they contribute to the well-being of our family and my peace of mind. I also honor my parents, Jim and Theresa Ramsey for building a firm and loving foundation.

Two friends helped me as gentle critics and supportive guides: Ann Kirkman and Anita Blackburn. They each offered me exactly what I needed and I thank them. Ann suggested that I consider publication. Anita was my partner in bringing this book to life. Without her technical knowledge and tireless energy, it might not have come together. Many thanks to Ann and Anita.

I also was aware of receiving Divine Telegrams throughout the years I worked on the manuscript. I thank and honor the Source of those telegrams.

Preface

I began making notes for *Divine Telegram* about 13 years ago. At that time, I was not writing a book but keeping notes about what I was learning. I began to have interesting spiritual experiences and made notes on those as well. Those experiences opened my mind and broadened my understanding. Often, as I reread my notes, I wondered how I had written passages that contained information that I was unaware I possessed. I do not believe that I did possess that information.

On the surface, it may seem that some of what I have written conflicts with the tenets of my early life as a cradle Episcopalian. But my experience has allowed me to integrate them rather seamlessly. I don't claim to have a lot of answers. What I have are questions which lead me to search for possible answers. I don't possess certitude but rather a continued search. Throughout the writing of *Divine Telegram*, I have continued to learn and to question. My spiritual education has vastly enriched my life. I hope others can open themselves to a similar experience and thus find some answers to the mystery of life.

Chapter 1

The Spirit World

My religions consists of a humble admiration of the
illimitable superior spirit who reveals himself in the
slight details we are able to perceive with our frail
and feeble minds.

--Albert Einstein

STEP INTO THE spirit world. There is no need to leave your earthly reality; merely rise above it. Allow a new consciousness to direct your being. Be guided by the *real you*, your spirit, that which is unaffected by earthly concerns and values.

I was recently at a garage to have my car worked on. The attendant at the counter greeted me kindly, took my keys, and offered me a seat. At that moment a large, striking, younger African-American woman approached the desk and received minimal courtesy. Not quite sure why, I struck up a conversation with her, commenting that it looked like she was not having her best day. She explained that she had brought in her mother's car for repair on her way to work. I suggested that she forget how the man had spoken to her and go out and have a wonderful day in spite of it. She uttered a phrase I will never forget. Smiling, she said, "I'm going to send out love no matter what I get back." After she left, I immediately wrote down her words so that I could practice the sentiment in my own life.

As my friend Gloria used to say, "I met an angel." The woman had taught me something, not only through her words but especially through her demonstration of putting those words into action. When the student is ready the teacher will appear. That woman lived her life on a spiritual plane, despite worldly influences and negative experiences. A smile had never left her face. I had received a divine telegram.

Our thoughts and words are powerful in our lives. They direct our behavior, initiative, perceptions, judgment, and even achievements. They even determine the status of our health. We are unlikely to achieve that which we feel unworthy or unprepared to achieve. If we attribute power and influence to the words and beliefs of others about ourselves, we give them power over us. In both cases, it is we who award the power and actually choose to give it. Through our thoughts, attitudes and expectations, we speak to the universe and bring about our own realities and influence or actually determine our futures.

The woman at the garage did not choose to give power to the words and behavior of the man at the counter. She knew who she was and she knew she was worthy whether or not someone else recognized it. She functioned on a spiritual level and she did not treat him with anything but respect. When I reached out she reached back to me. She remained joy-filled. She controlled her thoughts and emotions. Because she didn't allow the man to make her feel belittled, she had no anger or resentment. I feel confident that she did not fume on the drive to work, or cut other drivers off, or arrive at work angry and bitter. Nor did she spread negative feelings among her colleagues. She did not give away or relinquish her personal power. That woman is a mortal being who copes with the everyday challenges that we all do, but she lives her life on a spiritual plane. She is joy-filled. I sensed or felt that spirit from her in a way I rarely do from others. She radiated her spirit.

Our daily lives and work may subject us to slights and mistreatment. Occasionally, we are subjected to worse criticism, judgment, or prejudice. We have a choice. Will we react confrontationally with anger coursing through our bodies, adrenalin rushing to mount our counter attack?

Most of us have experienced road rage at one time or another. How we choose to react (the key word being *choose*), is a clear indicator of how much we have learned about handling negative emotions. At one end of the spectrum, a person may experience raw fury, physically confronting another car or driver by tailgating or blocking their passage, perhaps shouting or gesturing. That person may indeed have a history of over-reacting to negative experiences and may simply not yet know how to handle these experiences any other way.

In the middle of the spectrum, a person may experience anger that is internalized and may ruin the rest of the day and affect how the driver relates to others throughout the day. I admit that I spent a large portion of my life at this level of the spectrum. A new goal for dealing with an incident of road rage might be to get some emotional distance from the experience. If you're cut off in traffic, don't take it personally but see it for what it really is: angry, aggressive behavior on the part of the other driver. You must see it as just that and not internalize it. Don't make it about you. Perhaps you can tell yourself that it's just traffic and you're not going to react to it. View the other driver as acting out and refuse to join him.

Keep a cool head. Guide your conscious mind to what is great in your life; list a few of your many blessings, and not the negative that is happening at this instant. Repeat a mantra such as "It's just traffic; it doesn't bother me." Rather than giving in to an anger response, remind yourself what *is* important in your life. No doubt, traffic will be nowhere on that list.

Therapists often note that clients use "catastrophic language" to explain problems to themselves or others. A dear friend of mine frequently describes small accidents or incidents as "calamities." He perceives them as such and blows up their magnitude several hundred percent. This guarantees an emotional over-reaction. We have to be aware of how we view and how we describe our issues. If we internalize accidents and incidents as catastrophes, calamities, or disasters, we have unknowingly set ourselves up for an over-reaction. It is at such times that we have to find our backbones, brace ourselves, and deal with everyday life with calm confidence. I am convinced that emotional over-reactions to everyday stressors and aggravations can have horrible effects on our relationships, careers, and even on our physical and mental health.

Never underestimate the power of mantras or affirmations, thoughts to help us build the attitude we want to have. Plan those mantras in advance and learn them so they are available for use when needed. Often, when we are under stress and need the affirmations, they are less available unless they've been committed to memory. They help us train our thinking. Whether the goal is to break an addiction, lose weight, calm our thoughts, work harder, build our confidence, or overcome temptation, there's a mantra for that! Customize your own, based on your needs, perhaps along these lines:

- ⚘ I will remain cool, calm and collected.
- ⚘ I will react reasonably and keep my head.

✸ This situation does not directly affect me and I will remain detached.

✸ I am strong and able to deal with this situation.

✸ I feel good about myself.

✸ I love myself and others.

✸ This can be done and so I will do it.

✸ I am safe.

✸ The universe wants me to succeed. I want to succeed. I will succeed.

✸ I will send out love no matter what I get back.

✸ My body is healing itself.

✸ My mind is open. I am open.

✸ I am joy-filled. I am joyful.

✸ I prosper wherever I turn.

✸ Everything is working out for my highest good.

✸ Healing miracles are taking place throughout my body and mind.

✸ I am joy-filled and grateful for everyone and everything in my life.

❀ I ask; I believe; I receive.

❀ My health is golden!

❀ Doors of opportunity open to me daily.

❀ My friendships and relationships are deep and enduring.

❀ My body heals quickly and immediately.

❀ I am strong, active and healthy.

❀ Joy is my mission in life!

❀ Opportunity presents itself daily.

❀ I am deeply loved by family and friends.

❀ I am protected and feel safe always.

❀ I am surrounded by caring, loving people.

❀ I accept and love other people.

❀ I trust my Inner Being to lead me and guide me.

❀ I choose to live in JOY this moment and every moment.

❀ Daily I find new things I can do well.

❀ I have boundless energy.

❀ I am confident and comfortable in all situations.

If you have taken these affirmations to heart, if you have read them and taken them in, I believe you have already done your body a world of good. I believe that if you measure your blood pressure, it may have gone down and you may have a greater sense of peace. You are likely more open than usual. If you read these words with suspicious or a sense of rejection, these changes probably did not occur. You may have deprived yourself of them. Belief is the difference. What you believe you can achieve.

When stating affirmations, it is important to understand that our subconscious minds do not recognize negatives. So affirmations must be stated positively. Instead of saying, "I cannot fail," say "I will succeed." Instead of "I will never worry," say "I maintain peace of mind." Use no form of negatives in affirmations or in hypnosis because the subconscious will interpret a positive form of the statement, which is the opposite of your goal. Stay positive in all things! Consult works by Louise Hay to find a multitude of affirmations. Have them at the ready because during times of upset it may be difficult to plan an appropriate affirmation.

Affirmations also serve as intentions when read or said before taking action. Remind yourself of your intentions and your expectations. Before making a presentation or trying out or interviewing, review your affirmations several times if necessary: I am self-confident. I have valuable experience (or talent, ability, drive, skill, or initiative). I am strong, gifted, and capable. I totally believe in myself. Doors of opportunity are opening to me, even now. Opportunity presents itself daily. I am confident and comfortable in all situations.

Build your confidence and sense of well-being with affirmations. Design or customize them to your personal needs.

If you feel unsafe or vulnerable, build your inner peace with such affirmations as: I am protected and feel safe always. I trust my Inner Being to lead me and guide me. I listen attentively. I am blessed. All is well in my life. I move safely through this situation with assurance.

If you feel that your health or well-being is jeopardized, remind your body of its innate ability to heal itself: I am self-healing. I have boundless energy. I bless this beautiful, precious body of mine. I love it and I care for it. I send healing energy throughout my body. My body heals quickly and immediately and I am strong, active and healthy.

If you find yourself in a negative mood, change it immediately. The first step is to remind yourself of as many blessings as you can roll off your tongue. Then begin your affirmations: Joy is my mission in life! Joy and love! I am deeply loved by family and friends. My life is surrounded by caring, loving people and I show them care and love daily. I accept and love other people and this builds strong and enduring friendships and relationships. I send joy throughout my body.

If these sorts of affirmations ring hollow in your ear, or do not ring true, you have work to do. You must repeat them faithfully and come to believe them. You must repeat them and make them a part of your belief system and your consciousness. What makes these words powerful is your *belief* in them. Then you begin to live by these beliefs.

Your spirit wants the best things: peace, joy, harmony, to love and to be loved…the sweet things in life. If we keep our spirit in charge of our being, we will have those emotions. Perhaps that's what the phrase, "Rise above it" means. Don't get drug down by earthly pessimism, fear, and negativism or base human behaviors. If we're staying in spirit, does it mean that bad things won't happen to us? Probably not, much as we might wish it. Instead, how we confront those things will be spirit-filled. Our very thoughts, however, will influence our beliefs and behavior. Imagine that you've dropped a glass and broken it. Do you berate yourself? ("That was so stupid. What a horrible mess. I can't believe I was so dumb.") Or simply, 'Whoops!" That one word, "Whoops!" means so much: Things will happen. It's not a big deal. It was an accident. No need to blame. Move on. That one word is in itself the briefest of mantras!

In order to receive divine telegrams we must be living in spirit. They don't come to us as we berate ourselves and others, or find fault, criticize, belittle, or judge. We must be loving and open. We must bathe in joy and expectation.

Sometimes divine telegrams may come to you in your sleep, often just before waking. They may be literal messages, but are often figurative messages. Once, while my husband and I were visiting my daughter's home in Washington, DC, I awoke when I felt someone touching my upper arm. It was on the opposite side from where my husband was sleeping. I heard a voice urging me to "see a doctor." No, it was not an audible voice in the room, but it was a voice nonetheless. Because I heard it just as I was awakening, it startled and frightened me. I do not have complete recall about the tone of the voice, but I do recall being concerned. I comforted myself with the realization that I would not have received the warning if there were nothing I could do about it. At the time, I wondered if the voice was my deceased father's warning to care for myself, as he had always done in life. I also considered that it might be a voice from within: my body communicating with my mind, so to speak. I scheduled an appointment with my doctor as soon as I returned home. She found cancerous cells, scheduled surgery, and I am now healthy once again. I am healthy because *I received a divine telegram* and I acted on it. Was it my imagination? Possibly it was, although no one could ever persuade me of that. I experienced it. Where do divine telegrams come from? I don't have an answer for that, although I do have several ideas, as I am sure you do as well. For now, I don't choose to make a judgment about something I do not have real evidence to decide. I am just grateful that I received that particular divine telegram, and several subsequent telegrams as well.

I have spoken with and read about people who have received similar telegrams regarding creative matters, rather than health matters. There are reports of people composing entire songs in their sleep, receiving complete ideas for inventions, solving long-term problems in the blink of an eye with one mighty insight, receiving an inspiration for a work of art, receiving an entire plot for a novel, or a musical score. Some people receive the basic germ of an idea which they then have to develop during their waking hours. Others have received messages directing them to a career change. We can receive guidance and direction about any aspect of our lives merely by being open to it, welcoming it in whatever form it may appear. Guidance often comes from the most unlikely people. If we have a preconceived notion of who might give us insight or direction, we might miss it. The universe sends some unlikely messengers.

We also have to be in touch with our own consciousness. Our subconscious may attempt to communicate messages or information to our minds or bodies. This may happen during a dream state, during moments of distraction and day dreaming, or even during intense concentration. Being open to the message is the key. Before retiring at night, one might repeat the mantra, "Everything I need to know will be revealed to me." Upon awakening in the morning, quietly reflect on the images or thoughts that pervaded the sleeping hours. Keep a journal by the bed to record a few notes, if possible. Be open, night after night, to incoming messages, or divine telegrams. Then consider your expanded awareness and what action is appropriate, if any.

When you receive a divine telegram, you will want to recall every nuance and impression. Telegrams may even come to us in the form of symbols rather than words. Record notes about the message immediately after you awaken. Record memories, impressions, visions recollections, all in as great a detail as possible whether or not they all fit together logically. Do not immediately draw a conclusion, but consider the possibilities of any conclusions that come to mind. Think, reason, evaluate. I believe that we receive information from our subconscious, our spirit guides and from our Creator, using symbols that are personal to us, symbols that might be meaningless to someone else. My own experience has been that I am given information in a way that I can relate to it, using symbols that I am familiar with and that are meaningful to me personally. I had only to be open to them.

Chapter 2

Spiritual Attitudes

As you simplify your life, the laws of the universe will be simpler; solitude will not be solitude, poverty will not be poverty, nor weakness, weakness.

--Henry David Thoreau

OUR LIVES ARE becoming more and more complex. The complexity is often due to the most insignificant details of our existence, leaving us with less energy and less joy. If our mental awareness is focused on a perceived slight, looking for a parking space, worrying about an ache or pain, or dealing with our neighbor's or spouse's behavior, our energy is depleted. We may not stay in awareness that we are

18

living life. We may not focus on living it. We may not search for guidance. Life can then become an empty or mundane existence rather than the joy-filled adventure it is meant to be. Even those who live fast-paced lives of wild abandon and pleasure seeking may eventually come to realize their lives are empty. Many factors contribute to a meaningful and enjoyable life. One of these is certainly our career. When we choose a career, we do so for many reasons but primarily for two reasons: for our spirit to soar (or you may call it 'passion') and to provide for ourselves and our family. If either of those needs is unmet through our careers, we will experience dissonance or dissatisfaction which perhaps leads eventually to feelings of depression. It is not surprising that people who have not found the career that allows their spirits to soar experience feelings of sadness, frustration, and anger. They may feel trapped by economic circumstances or other pressures that keep them in a job that does not feed their soul. For some, these feelings are modified by having a hobby or creative endeavor that allows expression of the soul. As you reflect on any dissatisfaction that you may have in your job, it is critical to understand that you must take an active role in becoming satisfied. It is not something that is done to you while you sit passively at your desk or on the couch. You must carefully evaluate your performance and your attitude. Do you connect with others with an open heart? Do you always do what you know to be right and ethical? Are you, as Don Miguel Ruiz describes in his book *The Four Agreements*, "impeccable with your word"? Do you have the intention of serving others? If you do these things and still feel empty inside regarding to your career, it may be wise to thoughtfully and prayerfully ask for guidance. And, then you must do the hardest thing--wait. Continue to be in thought and expectation as you wait. The universe's time is not our time. God's time is not our time. I have generally felt that all things are possible, and I live my life as though it is so; it seems to be so. Life bears that out. Be patient knowing that all things are possible. Time and again I receive direction in a very spiritual way through *divine telegrams.* These telegrams come in many forms: intense yearning, vivid dreams, the words of a child or a stranger, sometimes a psychic push to do something I don't want to do, or even a nagging feeling that leads to discovery. These telegrams stop me in my tracks and force me to think, deliberate, pause, pray, and listen. It is the natural order of life. It is not strange or far-fetched; I find these experiences normal and reassuring. However, if there is a psychic dimension to these experiences that, too, is normal and healthy. I believe that our society is still in the Stone Age regarding understanding the capability of our psyches. We do not understand or utilize the full power of our minds.

There are, however, some things that interfere with receipt of the telegrams: constant use of electronic devices, noise, worry, obsession, anger, or busyness. We must make a space in life and in spirit to receive these telegrams. If life is uncluttered, it is far easier to receive spiritual messages. If you do not accept the possibility of spiritual messages, I think that you at least agree that if life is uncluttered, it is far easier to *think*. Few of us are clear on the differences between thoughts and spiritual messages. My belief is that spiritual messages come, not just from our own brains, but from a universal intelligence, be that God, our spiritual guides, or the vast knowledge of those who lived before us. It is difficult to quantify this belief except to say that I have been privy to guidance and knowledge that I did not possess. I believe that was because I was open to possibilities that I did not understand. George Bernard Shaw said, "Life is no brief candle for me. It is a sort of splendid torch which I have got hold of for the moment, and I want to make it burn as brightly as possible before handing it on to future generations." Our spirits are mighty and I don't believe that they ever cease to be.

If we frequently expose ourselves to the media (and who doesn't?), our thoughts and ideas may be shaped in pathological ways. We may be imbued with fear and fright over things that will almost certainly never come to pass in our own lives (tsunamis, flesh-eating bacteria, mad cow disease, volcanic eruptions). We witness people behaving in horrendous ways towards others and we feel as if we were eye witnesses. We may then be influenced negatively to make generalizations about our fellow human beings, perhaps to become highly suspicious and distrusting of others. But, by constant exposure to incredibly rare or unlikely negative events, our minds become polluted by fear or dread. This is hardly a nurturing state for our precious spirits, those entities that wish to fly free soaring above the realities and embracing the possibilities. Our minds were not meant to observe and witness all of the atrocities possible in the world. And yet, the electronic and digital media make that very witnessing not only possible but likely. We have to protect ourselves from such constant witnessing in order to nurture ourselves. As newspapers around the world succumb to bankruptcy, the future of news appears to lie primarily in the electronic and digital media which makes photographs, video, and firsthand witnesses readily available. How many of us have the images of 9/11 emblazoned in our memories as though we saw it all? We did see it. Our psyches do not easily differentiate between what we witness and what we experience ourselves. It's a psychological burden to see so many travesties in our mind's eye because we have been exposed to them in such a personal way.

We cannot expect to impact the avalanche of atrocities but we can refuse to be eye witnesses to them and, consequently, mitigate their harmful influences on us. The effect of controlling how much negative news we see and read is somewhat proportional to the joy we will experience in our lives. While not putting their heads in the proverbial sand, several of my friends--myself included--have chosen not to watch daily news accounts of shootings, abuse, and other tragedies. If we cannot positively affect such drastic situations, it does little good to be intimately informed of them. In addition, the less time we spend artificially living our lives or watching characters pretend to live life and substituting online friends for actual ones, the more valid, real, healthy, and fulfilling our own lives will be.

To some degree, we bring about things that we truly focus our minds on. Thoughts that occur frequently may become beliefs. Beliefs lead to action and behavior. Through real attention and focus we can give birth to our dreams. Even when we are not attentively focused on our dreams, our subconscious continues to labor away on dream fulfillment. Some attribute this to the Law of Attraction. When you make a real effort to focus your energy, amazing things begin to happen. It may be that we are aided in that fulfillment by the forces of the universe. It is a double-edged sword in that we can create reality by our thoughts and, because our thoughts may be negative, we then may create what we do not want. It is most important that we think on the positive and distract ourselves from the negative whenever possible. We all have to deal with negatives but it is very realistic to explain things to ourselves in a more positive and encouraging light. Negative thoughts and beliefs can damage our bodies. There is no need to wallow in tragedy via the nightly news coverage. Conversely, we can largely heal ourselves by our thoughts as well. Western culture has largely underestimated the power of our minds and of our thinking. Consequently, we have neglected to use our own powers. They may have atrophied. Some of us in the western world seem to lack the wondrous powers of concentration possessed by believers in the Far East. If you do not believe in your intuition, you almost certainly stifle it and therefore fail to benefit from and utilize it. I believe that the potential powers are present and we need to retool our beliefs and subsequently our abilities.

As I began to broaden my understanding and belief about what was possible, I began to surprise and then amaze myself at my expanded capabilities. I started small. First, I wanted to alleviate my reliance on sleep aids. After going to bed, I would program my mind with the behaviors I wanted. "I will go to sleep easily and quickly. I will fall into deep and comfortable sleep. If I have to wake up to go to the bathroom, I will fall asleep immediately after returning to bed. I will sleep until 5:30. My mind and body are comfortable and ready to sleep. I am grateful."

I had such positive results from my sleep experience that I began to request more of my mind and body. After breaking my foot and suffering the pain and inherent loss of freedom, I began to direct my body to heal itself. I threw my body and mind into total cooperation with that directive. "Even now, my foot is healing itself. My body and mind are causing my foot to heal. My energy is a healing energy. My body knows how to heal itself." The words are not powerful without the belief. In addition to my focus on the act of healing, I also focused on complete and accomplished health. I used such affirmations as "My foot is completely healthy. I am completely and totally health in every way." The belief and the faith are the healing energies. I have continued to heal myself in this manner, and I have continued to focus my attention almost exclusively on that which I DO WANT. In order to do so, I had to discipline my thinking which I suspect may be harder than stopping smoking!

Chapter 3

Receiving Divine Telegrams

The universe is transformation; our life is what our

thoughts make it.

--Marcus Aurelius

MANY OF OUR thoughts are burdensome or dysfunctional. A habit of negative thoughts and feelings may have negative effects on our cellular structure and on our immune system. Once we finally come to understand this, we cannot afford the luxury of a negative thought. Our emotional guidance system warns us away from negative thoughts by giving us feelings of distress. We must immediately exercise self-discipline and substitute a positive feeling for the negative thought. We do this time and time again until it becomes habit.

One of the descriptors of greatness is a disciplined mind. Many famous scientists, world leaders, and philosophers have discovered this. Require your mind to focus on positives. Require your mind to feel good! Your body will thank you and you will live a happier and healthier life.

During ancient days, the Indian philosopher Patanjali taught that "When you are inspired by some great purpose, some extraordinary project, all of your thoughts break their bonds: your mind transcends limitations, your consciousness expands in every direction and you find yourself in a new, great and wonderful world. Dormant forces, faculties and talents become alive and you discover yourself to be a greater person that you ever dreamed yourself to be." If you are engaged in some important undertaking that means a great deal to you, read Patanjali's words again and again and take them into your soul. His words are powerful indeed.

Perhaps you might copy them and carry them with you or post them above your desk.

There is an unfettered spirit that resides in each of us, complete with our God-given abilities and a knowing gained possibly over many lifetimes. Even if you do not accept that, could you merely accept the possibility? Many of us carry our earliest lessons with us throughout the rest of our lives. Often, this is a positive thing. But, occasionally it becomes a belief that is unaffected by change, experience, truth, or proof of any kind. If our minds are closed to new information and experiences, we cannot benefit from the lessons of life. Your experiences and your understanding provide a clear direction in choices you will make and in changing your behaviors and broadening your horizons. Mankind progresses; mankind does not stagnate on old beliefs and old information however useful they might once have been. I do not yet have a belief about whether or not we have lived before. Because I believe our souls live forever, I came to have an open mind about that issue. And I believe it is indeed possible.

Chapter 4

The Agreements

In a time of deceit, telling the truth is a revolutionary act.

--George Orwell

A FEW YEARS ago I drove to Topsail Isle to spend a few days alone in my friend Margie's beach house. I let myself in, unloaded the car, fixed a glass of wine and, at about 11 p.m., I began to read a book I found in a stack under the coffee table. I later learned that the book had been a gift to Margie as she successfully fought the fight of her life against breast cancer. I stayed up that night until I finished the last page of that life-changing book:

The Four Agreements. To this day, I continue to review the concepts in the book, always finding new application to my own life. It is amazing to me that I may skim over something in the book and, on a different day, find that very passage astounding, illuminating, and applicable to my own circumstances. I think this may be true of all of us; again, when the student is ready, the teacher appears.

In *The Four Agreements,* author Don Miguel Ruiz gives indispensable guidance that bears reflecting on each and every day. His ideas seem so simple and yet complex. He urges us to speak with integrity. You were taught as a child to tell the truth but are you, to use Ruiz's words, "impeccable with your word"? How many of us really are? Telling the truth may seem easy but being impeccable with our words is a lofty goal indeed. It may take a lifetime to achieve. I am well aware of the leap I am making here but I believe that if nations were impeccable with their word, and if they attended to the other three agreements as well, it could result in an entirely peaceful world. On a societal basis it would mean the end of stealing, fraud, cheating, subterfuge, and suspicion. If we all embraced the agreements, it would contribute mightily to a spirit-filled, more trusting world. Our relationships would be healthier. Even though the truth is not always lovely, it is real and valid; we would begin to recognize truth when we hear it and live by it. It would eliminate huge handicaps in family relationships, marriages, friendships, and world peace by eliminating manipulation, duplicity, and a trust deficit. In time, perhaps the need for national borders would disappear as the world becomes a family of man--the children of the universe. Change would start with individuals and the growth would be a phenomenon.

Recently I watched a televised interview with a government official. He answered each question directly and without subterfuge. I was startled to hear him making comments that were critical and yet upfront about his department's conduct and about himself. He then actually took responsibility for those actions and vowed to make subsequent changes. The man spoke from his heart. There was not a blending of facts and excuses. It did not seem to me that his department had deliberately done wrong, but that they saw errors in the procedures and were determined to do right. In awe, I realized that I was hearing the truth. It was a knowing. I did not consciously evaluate his words. I believe that either our bodies or our minds recognize the pure truth when unadulterated by slanting, excuses, and rewritten history. It may be, however, that we don't have a great deal of experience hearing it.

A human tendency is to put ourselves at the center of an issue--to personalize it. This is an egocentric behavior which distorts reality. Children do this habitually and naturally but, as adults, we hope to leave this tendency behind. When something becomes deeply personal to us, we then lose perspective on it. When we depersonalize an issue or an event, we may then regain perspective. Never think that someone else has done something because of you. Other people don't do things because of you. They do things because of something within them, some experience they have had, some belief that they hold. Let go of the tendency to make yourself the center of the universe.

Ruiz seems to consider that always doing your best is a form of truth. He stresses that this is a form of truth. You do your best to please yourself and, because it is right, not to please or impress others. The self-respect you experience is your compensation. If we all lived by this agreement, what a world change would occur.

The final agreement is interwoven with the others. It warns us that often we assume things that are very wrong, thereby distorting what we are seeing or hearing by so personalizing facts or circumstances that the actual truth is lost. Imagine, for instance, that someone writes a vague statement on Facebook. His or her Facebook friends may then begin personalizing the statement wondering if it's about them and perhaps needlessly taking offense. These sorts of misunderstandings take place across the culture: in schools, business places, and communities. The person making the initial statement is often blamed for things unintended. The reader or listener warps the original intent of the statement by taking it personally and perhaps by taking offense. If one lives by the agreements, needless pain and drama can be alleviated and communication enhanced.

Don Miguel Ruiz' four agreements may seem simplistic on the surface, however, nothing could be further from the truth. Each agreement has many layers of complexity. As we study each one and begin to integrate them into our lives, we become aware of the difficulty of changing our habits and our thinking. But the reward is immense! As we build self-respect and confidence, we lose fear and confusion.

I received two divine telegrams in relation to Ruiz's book. As my older daughter and I were driving to the beach, I began to tell her about his book and about the agreements. She listened carefully and commented and questioned; we had an excellent discussion. The following day as we entered a massage therapy spa, there was one solitary item on the table in the lobby: the inspiration cards for *The Four Agreements*! I don't really believe in coincidences. That experience underlined for both of us the application of the book and its illustrated cards and made it more meaningful to our lives. I considered that the second telegram about the importance of the agreements to my life and to my family. I marvel at how the universe gets your attention and then puts an accent on it in case you failed to understand the implications. The universe merely requires that we be open to communication and insight. If we restrict our beliefs to only those which we were taught or came to believe early in life, we have cut ourselves off from learning and growing. Is it incomprehensible in the western world that our souls could live more than one life? Could our very souls also continue to live and to learn and benefit from experience? Are you open to that possibility?

Chapter 5

Your Emotional Guidance System

Let each man take the path according to his capacity,

understanding and temperament. His true guru will

meet him along that path.

--Sivananda Saraswati

FOR MANY, ANXIETY or fear can be crippling. The numbers of people who are medicated to deal with life are staggering. Often, medication may be the best solution but often we can bring about peace of mind and serenity ourselves.

What we imagine is more real to us than actual reality. We concoct innumerable things to fear, both as a society and individually. We cannot change those thoughts until we become aware of them. Mark Twain said it best, "I have known a great many troubles, but most of them never happened."

In the 21st century, most of us spend far too much time in our heads. The body can help us cope with our emotions. As a counselor, I used to feel my body reacting to stressful counseling sessions. If my client disclosed a terrible loss, I might feel my heart rate increasing, my body stiffening, and my blood pumping. I learned early to trick my body into relaxing. I did this by leaning back in my chair, assuming a relaxed posture, unclenching my fists, and breathing deeply. When I was alone during tense or worrisome experiences, I would even yawn and stretch! These actions served to remind my body that I was not experiencing the situation being described. I was then able to keep a perspective that allowed me to think, reason, and react properly. I was able to keep my attention on the client's needs.

When you are in a tense and stressful situation or experiencing fear or panic, sit down and put your full attention on your body instead of your mind. Deepak Chopra describes this as getting out of your mind and back into your body.

- ❀ Focus on your body.

- ❀ Breathe deeply.

- ❀ Sip water if available. Dab some on your face as you breathe deeply.

- ❀ Lower your shoulders and feel your neck and back relaxing.

- ❀ Lean back in your seat as you lower your chin to your chest.

- ❀ Slowly stretch.

- ❀ Yawn. Sigh contentedly. Trick your body into relaxing by assuming the behaviors your body engages in when you are truly relaxed.

- ❀ Quit striving; stop the constant goal setting and never-ending reaching.

❀ Embrace satisfaction.

❀ Understand the concept of 'enough'.

Constant striving sets up within us a sometimes never-fulfilled sense of desire. Simplicity is our natural state. The ideal is to have what we need but not to be overwhelmed by *stuff*. The Japanese have set an example that much of the western world has refused to follow: simple lifestyle, simple homes, simple needs, and simple decor. There is beauty in simplicity. One perfect rose may be preferable to a dozen, if you choose to see it that way. One single rose beginning to lose its petals may be more beautiful than the perfect rose because it reflects reality and the circle of life. It is up to each of us to reflect on why this might be. It is a paradox that this is a new (and yet ancient) way of thinking. It may even be the lesson of the global recession we are experiencing. The opposite of simplicity is *greed*. It may not seem so on the surface but, when we cannot achieve simple satisfaction in our goals, lifestyle, or achievements, we may find ourselves in a never-ending cycle of greed:

work more, achieve more, possess more, out-race and out-own others. Perfectionism holds hands with depression. Being a perfectionist sets one up for depression because one can never be perfect however hard one tries. In the same way, constant striving sets one up for an unsatisfied life. The solution is equally simple: ENOUGH! You almost assuredly have enough clothes, enough knick-knacks, enough goals, enough cars and, yes, though you probably don't realize it and may deny it, even enough time. What you do not have enough of are experiences! My wish is that you find satisfaction in what you have, who you are, and what you have learned so far. Perhaps you might utilize some of those attributes and gifts differently and adjust your own expectations. In fact, three weeks generally form the solution to most of life's problems. Do two things: wait patiently and adjust your expectations. The latter, adjusting your expectations, is the key to resolving most of life's dilemmas. Our expectations (of our children, our jobs, our mates, our physical appearance, the party we are hosting, the project we are working on) are heightened by our observations of others and influenced by some of the near perfection we see portrayed on television or read about. They are unrealistic and, furthermore, they set us up for disappointment. Our only comparisons should be based on ourselves: How am I doing compared to yesterday? How can I improve? Am I beating my own record? Do I like what I've created?

Don't envision perfection; it is an illusion. Value life as it is. Value yourself, children, family, friends, career, and home as they all truly are. The only thing that needs to be perfect is your satisfaction.

The more satisfied you are with your life, with your career, home, and family, the more physically healthy you will be. If you are dissatisfied, don't leap to changing your job, house, or spouse! Change your estimation of these aspects of your life. Change how you value them and yourself. Change your level of demands from others. Change your expectations of what life should be; change your material requirements, and change your perspective.

Find joy in what you now have. Expand your gratitude and

your joy. Your satisfaction about you and your life will

expand exponentially.

Chapter 6

The Spirit and the Body

The superior man will watch over himself when he is alone. He examines his heart that there may be nothing wrong there, and that he may have no cause of dissatisfaction with himself.

--Confucius

AT TIMES, MOST of us battle sadness, distress, or regret. For some, it may become depression; others keep it at bay. The happiest among us refuse to experience dissatisfaction, or we reframe it into an experience from which we may benefit. The gratitude journal is a very real tool for focusing our attention on the positives and understanding how we are blessed. It is much harder to feel down after one has listed and documented the blessings of the day. I suggest you list small, seemingly inconsequential, things for which you are grateful, as well as the large blessings such as home, family, career, and good health. If you begin to really value the small pleasures in life: the taste of chai tea, the raindrops outside the window, your spouse's care and concern (hardly a little thing), a heart-to-heart talk with a friend, a piece of useful advice, an improvement, the Sunday paper, new buds on a tree, fresh herbs in your salad the possibilities are limitless that you will notice things you took for granted and failed to value. If you've experienced painful times: a sad childhood, a life of deprivation, disease, a lost job, an addiction, betrayal, a loss, a difficult divorce, failure--it is understandable that you did not view those as blessings. Realize that others have turned those negative experiences into challenges to overcome, springboards to a fuller life, reasons to achieve; you can as well. Adjust your perspective; take a new view and reframe the experience. How has it changed you? Be your own therapist and discuss these things aloud or in a journal. Ask yourself questions. How do I feel about this experience now? What can I take from it and use to rebuild my life? How have I benefited from it? What would I have been like if I had not learned this life lesson or had this experience? If another individual has caused you great pain, have a conversation with that person in your mind or do it aloud. Envision the person sitting in a chair in the room. Talk. Recount your recollections. Describe your feelings, both at the time of the abuse and now. Tell the person how you are overcoming his or her actions or abuse. Offer your forgiveness, the most important thing you can do for your own spirit. If any of this seems impossible for you to do, consider seeing a therapist who will help you crystallize your life experiences and either cope or benefit from them.

Another experience for enhancing your ability to find gratitude in simple things is to describe how the world is different because you live in it. What impact have you had on others? What lives have you enriched and how? Don't neglect the small things. Part of this exercise is to learn to value those small things. Those many small things can add up to a tidal wave of blessings! There is an unexpected irony in this exercise; often the people we have helped the least value our help more than those we have done the most for. I hope you do not let this dictate your actions, however. Just accept it as a natural law or even unnatural law. For what you do for others should never be predicated on their reciprocation. In doing things anonymously (rendering aid, giving assistance, donating, helping others), our spirits truly thrive. Though our conscious minds may not recognize that giving without recognition or reward is true generosity, our spirits certainly do. For I believe that this is what we are on earth to do--care for others, care for ourselves, and to love life.

If our energy is diverted to the accumulation of a vast amount of resources, titles, or achievements, if our goal becomes surpassing others, achieving promotions, and accruing material wealth, it is almost certain that we are not living in spirit while we may also be defeating the goals of living and diminishing our energy.

To be fully joyful and engaged in life, it is extremely important to have a healthy body. Let's begin or continue to believe that we influence our health by our beliefs as well as our actions. Let's also understand the influence of our environment on our bodies and on our physical health. Let's live on purpose and with purpose.

Chapter 7

Being Open

The possibilities of creative effort connected with the

subconscious mind are stupendous and imponderable.

They inspire one with awe.

--Napoleon Hill

PERHAPS YOUR BODY is trying to send you a Divine Telegram. What is your body telling you? Are you listening? This is another reason to put aside time to be alone and to listen. Your subconscious, or perhaps it is your inner voice (your much older, much more experienced spirit), has important messages for you. Listen to the wisdom that escapes your conscious mind during the maelstrom of daily life and activity. Our brains have more information about our bodily systems and conditions than any of us realize. The trick is to tap that information, which is not at the ready or on the surface of our conscious minds. It is deeply hidden, more deeply hidden than the name of your third-grade teacher or your first telephone number. Our brains have more multitasking to do than it can efficiently do with prompt recall. To convince yourself of this, pause for a minute and pretend that you are driving down the highway. Your hands should be on the imaginary steering wheel. Now, move into the left lane. Did your hands move the wheel slightly to the left? Don't cheat yourself out of this experience. Try it! That's not how we change lanes! Your brain knows that we move the wheel slightly to the left and then back slightly to the right to straighten up. Thank goodness your subconscious is fully aware of that movement and has rehearsed it thousands of times and communicates the message to your hands. Try the experiment on a friend. The conscious mind, on the other hand, may be scanning the print ahead to find what's there or trying to decide whether to participate in the activity or just continue reading. Simultaneously, your conscious mind may be deciding whether to have coffee or tea, deciding whether to walk the dog before the day gets any warmer, or assessing whether you need more air in your tires. What a lengthy list of responsibilities has the brain! At times your conscious brain may cheat you out of rich experiences by urging you to take shortcuts, to not try something new, or to be disdainful of engaging in some activity. It may cause you to hesitate or reject making a connection with a new person. It may make you feel some doubts about yourself, and it may slow you down in taking action of any sort. Your subconscious brain is far more fun!

Your brain has its finger on the pulse (a strangely mixed metaphor) on everything that is happening in your body. The difficulty appears to be in communicating that information to the conscious mind which, if receptive, would have the option of taking action and making needed changes. Scientists are not yet able to measure and assess the vast abilities of the brain. Few people, especially in western culture, are yet open to the possibilities of all that the brain can do and, therefore, they do not require those abilities of their own brains. It may be this very disbelief that disables those functions. The solution is clear; choose to believe in the ability of your brain to perform heretofore unacknowledged tasks and thus enable your brain to handle them!

When you are called upon to make a decision, pay attention to how your body feels when you consider one option versus another. Give it some time and your complete attention; set no time limit. Our minds work at their own rates. Ideas and impressions come to the surface, perhaps in the form of the telegram, generally after we are fully engaged in something else: driving, swimming, hiking, sleeping, or reading.

When you require in-depth understanding of your child, spouse, or business partner, focus your attention on that person's recent and distant behavior and search for understanding. Insights may not come quickly. They often need to marinate before they gel, coming slowly to the surface of your understanding. How often I have wished for the gelling to come quickly and on demand. Alas, the mind appears to have its own timetable. I find the same is true of the universe. I don't receive information, opportunities, or guidance when I ask for it. It comes after I have almost abandoned ship and moved on!

Trust your innate knowledge and intuition to act as a guide in trusting people, making choices, and navigating life. Allow your mind and your psyche the time necessary to assess the situation and respond appropriately. Then be willing to be guided by it. This psyche is your inner self, an older and wiser self who can be trusted to guide you. The soul does not die. I believe that it may have lived before and is eternal. The soul is you--the true you. He or she (but probably has no gender or race) is with you always and has been with you always. The inner self communicates with us in one of the most reliable, clear and concise ways possible through the emotions. If you feel negative emotions while speaking, thinking or acting, you have just been warned away from the topic of those specific behaviors. Do not speak, think or act as you have just done. The message is clearly decipherable. Perhaps you have just verbalized a negative thought. You begin to feel unhappy or fearful. That feeling is your warning that the thought and its expression are damaging to you. Replace it immediately with a positive thought. Have ideas in advance so that you're prepared to replace thoughts of problems, complaints, or disease with ones of comfort, relaxation, love, or joy. When you have self-critical thoughts, visualize a STOP sign and immediately replace them with one such as mistakes are a great learning experience for me; I have benefitted from them. When you feel hurt or criticized by others, replace with one such as: While others may not approve, I am a unique individual and entitled to my own feelings and beliefs. If you feel fearful or apprehensive, replace with one such as: I feel confident in my ability to handle whatever I need to. Together with the Divine and my inner voice, we are a mighty team! Formulate a personal habit of catching a negative thought or idea and immediately replacing it with a positive thought. Frequent thoughts become beliefs. Examine your beliefs as they occur to you and revise them as necessary. Perhaps you could conclude positive thoughts with: All is well. (Never one for understatement, my own personal conclusion is: All is well and all is well!)

Chapter 8

Your Spirit Expressing Itself

We are spirits clad in veils.

--Christopher Pearse Cranch

HOW DOES YOUR spirit express itself? Does it have a means of expression? While I am still discovering my own expression of spirit, I seem to have more comprehension of the expression of my friends and family than I do my own. That would probably be true of most of us. A doctor wouldn't operate on himself and a lawyer who represents himself, as they say, has a fool for a client. We all need separation and a different perspective to judge ourselves.

But let's use the word 'assess' rather than 'judge', since often judging is done without kindness or compassion. Sometimes we can be especially unkind to ourselves. Another word for that is 'self-sabotaging.' What is your spirit's means of expression? Some of those methods of expression you may consider are activities or hobbies rather than the expression of spirit. But I think they are often the same. While one person may cook in order to get dinner on the table to nourish the family, another may cook with artistry and skill, making a delicious and appealing meal that warms the very soul or is artistry in its presentation. One or both of those may be an expression of spirit. Others might include music, dance, design, painting, sculpture, mosaics, choreography, mountain climbing, gardening, boating, writing, photography, learning, travel…the list is endless. Our spirits need to express themselves and they may choose several paths. They need freedom, nurturance, and acceptance. That acceptance must come from *us*. I view the human spirit as being somewhat childlike, but with the wisdom of an old soul. Don't stand in its way; give it free rein. Let it fly!

How do you nourish your spirit? Are there ways that your spirit appears to express itself? Are you willing to give it free reign and set it free? How would you go about doing that? You might start by encouraging yourself to dream as you are about to fall asleep. You may tell yourself, "I am going to dream tonight. My dreams will be vivid. They will tell me what I need to know. I am open to learning. In the morning, I will vividly recall my dreams." Keep a pad by your bed to record details upon awakening. Truly reflect on what you have dreamed and on what you have written.

Your spirit is not nourished by sitting on the couch watching imaginary characters live an imaginary life on television. While most of us have the habit to some degree or another, in excess it is a detriment to our quality of life.

You could spend some solitude time in nature. Listen to quiet music or sounds with your eyes shut. Write or type whatever comes to your mind and as fast as you possibly can and for as long as you can. That is your subconscious talking to you, a sort of shadow of the spirit. It is a marvelous way to be in touch with your true self. The subconscious is the true self, unaffected, uninfluenced, unadulterated by our culture. Give freedom to your spirit! Nurture it.

- ❀ Imagine
- ❀ Dream
- ❀ Think
- ❀ Wonder
- ❀ Pray
- ❀ Meditate
- ❀ Listen
- ❀ Create
- ❀ Dance
- ❀ Play

I think that the soul's greatest expression is through service. It could be a fundamental need and we would benefit by looking for ways to fulfill that need. We would not have to look very hard! Your job is to give your soul opportunity of expression. Throw wide the door! View your soul as flying across the sky, leaping and diving, skipping and gliding. Ask your soul what it wants to do next. Then give it your blessing and go along for the ride! Ask your soul what it wants to create. Give it your full cooperation, and give it time, as much time as is required. Don't rush the process. You wouldn't rush your child in learning to walk. We have fledgling little souls that need nourishment, encouragement, freedom, and time! Remember, spirit time is not our time.

As you read this, are you saying to yourself that your life, job, career, family, and responsibilities do not allow time for such expression? If you say this to yourself, consider this: You may have bought into or been driven into the cacophony, hubbub, tumult, rat race, pressure-cooker lifestyle. I'm not urging you to escape it. Redesign it, perhaps. Reallocate. I am only urging you to sit and think, walk and think, sleep and think, think and think and decide how to design the life you wish to live. Then, prepare and act on it. Your wise and reasoned decision must lead to wise action.

It is highly desirable to keep a meditative journal perhaps combined with a dream journal. Once you have the discipline of immediately recording your dreams and your subsequent thoughts and interpretations of those dreams, some astounding revelations may come into your conscious mind. This is all part of having an examined life. In the western world, many time-tested and enduring philosophies are given short shrift. Examples include the third eye, chakras, energy fields, psychic healing, and astral communication. These may be considered far out but I urge you to examine these concepts. The mind is capable of far more than we know. Study and experience have led me to astounding revelations, most after the age of 50. I'm a slow learner! I cannot imagine having lived my whole life without delving into these subjects and applying these skills to my life and my afterlife. If you believe in intuition, then you are well on your way to accepting other cosmic possibilities. If you have ever slept and dreamt, then you have had an out-of-body experience. If you have ever known what your partner was thinking or had a sense of foreboding that your child needed your help, then you have already acknowledged that your mind is capable of great things. Open yourself to possibilities.

We are spiritual beings and our human bodies are very transitory. Like cicadas, we continue to live after the disposal of our bodies. The Earth is our classroom, and there may well be other classrooms.

I hope there comes a day soon that we cease feeling fearful or dreadful about death. My firm belief is that death is merely the closing of this particular chapter, one in which our soul had goals to accomplish or roles to play in the lives of others. Please do not expect me to offer a complete explanation of death; I am unable to do so. What I can offer is a knowing, a confidence, that I hope you will come to feel after you eradicate your fears and negativity. We absolutely love our lives. We love the people in our lives. We love the joy we feel and the experiences we have. We love the sensual experiences our bodies deliver. We laugh, drink wine, smell flowers, hold babies, behold beauty, have sex, and eat delicious food. We do not want the chapter to close until we have squeezed out every drop of living! Live your life and be relaxed. All is well (and all is well).

Chapter 9

The Practice of Meditation Takes Practice

Meditation brings wisdom; lack of meditation leaves ignorance. Know well what leads you forward and what holds you back, and choose the path that leads to wisdom.

--Buddha

MEDITATION IS THE key to the development of the sixth sense and the third eye. Breath is the energy or the path by which energy flows. Breath is indeed the energy of life. Why is it hard for you to believe that you have an inner self? It is the 'you' that is unaffected by the values of our culture. It is the 'you' that emanated from our Creator, untouched by other influences. It is a part of the whole of the universe. It is your spirit which will live forever, your immortal soul.

Through meditation you can be touched and guided by your spirit and by our Source. It can be a conversation between you and the universe, a conversation to your benefit. As Louise Hay describes it, "Inner wisdom guides me at all times. Deep at the center of my being, there is a well of wisdom. All the answers to all the questions I shall ever ask reside there. This inner wisdom is connected to the vast wisdom of the Universe." We must train ourselves to be open to the guidance. We must learn to center ourselves and calm our minds. In prayer, we talk to God; in meditation, God talks to us.

When I first began meditating, my inner chatter had a comment on everything. It was also that inner chatter that was the source of my sleep problems. I found it very challenging to calm my mind in order to meditate. It was as though some aspect of myself refused to be open to growth.

There were times I thought I would never succeed. He urges us not to demand perfection in our meditations. Instead we should be patient with ourselves as we gradually learn to tune out the inner dialogue. It takes a great deal of practice, especially for those of us in the West.

Meditate daily with hope, with expectation. Meditate outside or where you can feel the breezes or hear water sounds if possible. Rain yourself to disregard noises and disturbances. Keep your eyes closed and stay in the zone. Try to gather your energy and send love to people and groups of people. Examples: Today I send love and healing to all people in hospitals and nursing homes. Then focus your attention on those people and will your love and healing energy to help them. Today I send love and healing to children who are victims of abuse. When you board a bus, a train, or a plane, send your loving energy out for the driver or pilot and for each passenger. Bless each individual passenger that you see. Let your intention be to send love and healing energy out to the universe. The universe is empowered by our loving energy and particularly so when we meditate in groups. John of God, the iconic Brazilian whose physical body is said to be inhabited by entities who publicly perform both physical and psychic surgeries on people, relies on group currents composed of people meditating together and sending out loving and healing energies. The group prayer and meditation energy creates the current, is said to empower the entities and to allow them to vibrate at our level, a level to facilitate healing. I am quite aware that healing in this way may be amazing and disturbing to many. However, it has been done in other cultures for centuries. Medical science now, however, possesses the methods of assessing the levels of success of psychic healings. At least, please accept the power of meditation used in these currents to focus a group of people on the single intention of bringing about the highest good for all. The entities (who were said to be medical doctors when they were alive) maintain that the healing comes from God, using the energy of the patient, the meditators, and the entities themselves. Without the faith of the patient, healing is not possible. The entities particularly welcome M.D.s to view the healing up close and to verify it.

At the Casa in Abadiania, Brazil, where John of God does his work, people are effectively trained in meditative practice so that they can participate in the current believed to facilitate the work of John of God and the Entities. Members of the current are generally those being healed. If you were a member of the current, you would be taught to (in their words):

- have a clear intention to put aside the ego and to use spiritual energy to create healing and transformation
- love yourself, other people, and all living beings in order to invoke divine energy
- harmonize your energy with the spiritual energy of others
- allow your spiritual energy to merge with the spiritual energy of others

- ❀ learn how to focus intention in order to transform energy in the group
- ❀ concentrate your efforts on holding your intention to bring love, harmony and union into the environment
- ❀ use the power of your imagination to believe that you are part of creating the healing space

If you discipline yourself to the practice of meditation, it will begin to serve you in untold ways. It is an expansion, not only of the mind, but of the self. Gradually, it will become as necessary to you as sleeping.

Add meditation to your arsenal of problem-solving tools. In time, I predict that it will become one of your most often utilized methods for calming yourself, gathering your wits about you, clarifying your ideas, and for giving birth to new ideas. It will sharpen your perspective about every aspect of life. It will bring you the guidance and energy you need in proceeding with your plans and ideas. It will help you to de-stress and eliminate guilt, anger, and resentment giving you a new dimension in living, one that is almost as critical as eating and sleeping. It will lift your spirits, bringing you inner peace. Make time for meditation; it is the energy of the soul. And fundamentally, it is the work of the soul.

Can you imagine the potential for mass meditation on our world? Perhaps it would accomplish nothing more than achieving a relaxed and centered population. On the other hand, might it be possible to bring about a universe that strategically solves problems of health and healing, eliminates starvation, solves economic dilemmas, and ends warfare.

Chapter 10

Living with Passion

Generosity is giving more than you can, and pride is
taking less than you need.

--Kahlil Gibran

OUR SPIRITS ARE nourished by our passions. Nourishment can come in many forms. One of the most powerful of these is generosity. Giving to others is not only noble, it is indispensable to the spirit. It is what we must do in order to truly live in spirit. A spirit that receives without giving is unbalanced. If you have more than you absolutely need, then you have certainly received. In our materialistic society, our spirits must avoid giving in order to receive recognition or reward. We must give out of sheer generosity, and give-- not until it hurts--as the saying goes, but continually. We give because we see a need and we need to help meet that need on behalf of someone else. Rather than thinking in terms of giving money or resources, think in terms of giving a blessing just as you have received blessings. Give, and then let it go, without expectation of recognition. Recognition is its own reward, so it may even create an imbalance. But let's abandon measurement and just give from the depths of our being; give with love and caring; give with the understanding that what we give is a blessing to others and consequently to ourselves. We bless others by giving of our time, attention, a listening ear, a favor, our organs, and in a myriad of ways. Nothing is too small to give. Whether or not your gift is appreciated does not matter to your spirit. What matters is that you offered the gift and gave of yourself. If your gift is not valued, practice the one exercise that will keep you grounded throughout life: adjust your expectations but never quit giving.

Somewhere on this earth, enough crops are being grown and food produced to feed every hungry person on this planet. The fact that we have hunger and starvation is not due to the earth being unable to meet the needs of its inhabitants. Hunger and starvation are due to some people taking far, far more than they could possibly need, perhaps out of a spirit of unhealthy competition. Once I believed that excess and greed in some members of society has guaranteed the starvation and need of others around the world and that if some people exhaust the resources of the world, then others will not have the necessary resources of life. I'm rethinking that and have not drawn a firm conclusion. I feel that the universe is capable of providing all that we need, and all that we ALL need. Still, it is the responsibility and solemn duty of each of us to preserve resources and to share and care for our precious island home. We must share our knowledge and expertise as well as our resources. We share, not in order to receive a tax deduction, an award, or a headline, but because what we have is in excess of what we need, and others need it! If we receive notoriety and gratitude, perhaps that is its own reward. I prefer a more spiritual reward, the knowledge that I've given what was needed.

As the worldwide recession gradually reduces worldwide resources hopefully, only on a temporary basis, sharing becomes vital. Waste becomes unacceptable. Values become clearer. Perhaps "McMansions" and a fleet of cars will become less desirable, replaced by food co-ops, gardens, and small efficient homes.

Churches in the United States often set great examples for meeting the needs of those who need assistance. Generosity of spirit is often alive and well in churches and houses of worship. Sometimes, however, well-intentioned people make decisions that cost others dearly. I'm concerned about the wealth of resources going into building church after church, accompanied by massive empty parking lots throughout the week, on once fertile land that could be farmed to feed the masses and shelter and feed wild animals. Could these buildings not also be shared? Could several congregations not share a building at different times? I love to read stories of people who form cowboy churches or neighborhood churches and meet in someone's barn or home, backyard, or under the trees! In the early days of the United States, buildings were used as schoolhouses during the week, churches on the weekend, and government meetings in the evenings. It's time for us to think differently and make decisions that preserve rather than expend resources. The first step is to actually recognize waste when we see it. That is not the easy step it appears to be because some members of society are so indoctrinated to waste. It is almost a societal descriptor and one that must change for the good of the globe.

One thing is certain, the global economy is changing. Need is increasing globally. We are being challenged. We may have brought the challenge to our own doorstep. We will learn to conserve, share, repurpose, downsize, and lower our expectations. We will adapt and we will change.

Chapter 11

The Power of Forgiveness

To forgive is to set a prisoner free and discover that

the prisoner was you.

--Lewis Smedes

A PRACTICE THAT is absolutely vital to our spirits is forgiveness. I do not believe that our spirits can evolve without learning forgiveness. If there is one essential aspect in the actualization of the spirit, I believe it is to learn to forgive and to forgive quickly.

If you have great resentment, anger, or a grudge against someone, you become bound to that person in a very real way. He or she may be completely unaware of it, but you may be tortured by that relationship. You may spend a large portion of your valuable life in experiencing emotional pain, agonizing about how you were treated or how unfair the person was to you. If you do this long enough or often enough, you may cause yourself actual physical pain or illness. In a manner of speaking, you have bound yourself to that person or perhaps even enslaved yourself. And why? Because you chose (yes, chose) to resent, to become angry, and to nurture those negative feelings long term. Refuse to be a prisoner any longer. Choose to forgive. Abandon the anger and resentment and the rumination over being mistreated. Tell that person or don't tell them, but *forgive* them. Then move on through your life without looking back over your shoulder. Perhaps you are now coming to the realization, if you had not done so earlier, that this life is not necessarily fair. We don't yet know about the next life. It is best for your well-being that you know and accept it so that you are not constantly disappointed or angry.

The seemingly unfair things that happen to us are part of a greater plan that we are unable to comprehend. Perhaps we are being tested or strengthened; we do not yet know. Meditate on this: We must proceed through life, overcome the hardships, mistreatment, and immense challenges while enjoying the great gifts and benefits and wonderful blessings that we have been offered. Don't forget to recognize those blessings as they come and to show gratitude.

In fact, our spirits are so intent on forgiving that, if we do not consent to forgive, our likelihood of developing physical illness is magnified many times. I see it as a sort of warfare between the conscious and the subconscious. Perhaps you have heard people say that when they chose to forgive, they did it for themselves rather than for the person they forgave.

When someone says that they will forgive but they will not forget, they just invalidated their words. They may not be aware that they have not forgiven and do not intend to.

Many benefits come to those who have chosen to forgive. Primarily, they will have fewer episodes of anxiety, depression and chronic pain. They will dramatically lower their stress and blood pressure. They may see their other relationships improve as the chip is removed from the shoulder. They will be less likely to self-medicate with alcohol or drugs. Finally, they will gain a sense of well-being, the reward to those who

- ❀ choose to forgive appears to be in regaining their own
- ❀ choose quality of life, and eventually their satisfaction and joy.

There is a strange paradox in forgiveness. The person who has deeply hurt or wronged you may not, strictly speaking, be deserving of forgiveness. Yet forgive you must, and for your own sake. Let go of anger and resentment. Open your heart. Let it all go.

Refusing to forgive others, while holding grudges and resentment, are seeds for disease, or disease. It is not in the best interest of others either, and it truly pollutes our world, sending harmful negative energy out to others. When we forgive wrongs and those who have done wrong it restores peace and joy to the world, or at least to our corner of it. Letting go of the bitterness that often accompanies the question of forgiveness must not have conditions in place for the sake of our own bodies and psyches.

Forgive immediately. Forgive freely and unconditionally. Then revel in your freedom! This is a *divine telegram* to anyone who carries the crippling burden of blame and resentment. Make the decision at this moment to wipe the slate clean. Then your life and your joy will begin and you will truly warrant the forgiveness that you yourself seek. Mahatma Gandhi warned us that "The weak can never forgive. Forgiveness is the attribute of the strong."

Chapter 12

Thinking in a "Certain Way"

To everyone is given the key to heaven; the same key

opens the gates of hell.

--Ancient Proverb

SHIFT YOUR AWARENESS toward positives. Cast out harmful thoughts, blame, resentment, grief and worry. Trust your body to remain healthy. Give it the means to do so, nutritionally and through movement. You cannot afford to have a negative thought because it will attract other negative thoughts and could end in a downward spiral. Instead, reverse the process and immediately replace it with an uplifting idea. I have found that the evening news has become my worst enemy, so I've chosen to rarely expose my mind to it. I can still read the newspaper and online news because I can skip over articles with appalling or negative headlines. If I learn of a crime, I say a silent prayer for the victims but I don't delve into the details. For many years I was a news junkie and read multiple papers, both physical and online, and would watch extensive news coverage. It was clear to me that I was paying a physical price for it, as well as losing what I treasure so much--peace of mind. Now, when my husband is watching the evening news, I am in the next room reading by the fireplace and relaxing. He used to call out, "Did you hear that?", but he no longer bothers. He will sometimes come to share his outrage at what he's heard, but I cannot share that any longer. I hope and believe that he may choose not to bathe in the bad news soon. It took me a long time to make that choice for myself. Some people are not as affected by the woes of others, and do not let it invade their personal space, and I believe that may be true of him.

But if you know that you are an empath, you may choose to avoid that negative stimulation.

When you feel an ache or pain, don't immediately jump to dramatic conclusions about illness. Make a choice to restructure your thoughts. Use an affirmation such as: I need to work that kink out. I'm sending a healing white light throughout my body. I am well. All is well. My body is strong and can resist anything. My health is golden! I am healing even now.

I recommend that you acquaint yourself with EFT, Emotional Freedom Techniques, a system of tapping on acupuncture points while orally addressing an emotional or physical issue developed by Gary Craig during the mid-nineties. While based on traditional Chinese medicine, there is still dissension about its value, however, whether due to science or the placebo effect, a distraction from physical pain or emotional trouble, it's efficacy with many people is undeniable. The theory is that EFT releases energy blockages that may have resulted in emotional issues. I have employed it and use it along with other methods. I suggest that you consider including EFT as one tool in your arsenal. Some EFT practitioners include some left- and right-brain activities (humming, singing, counting, shifting the gaze left and right). I have found this valuable. You may perform the method easily on yourself. It is not complex to learn. Many You Tube videos demonstrate EFT.

If you are familiar with The Law of Attraction, you may also be familiar with some of its earlier practitioners, which, according to Rhonda Byrnes, author of *The Secret,* include Shakespeare, Plato, Newton, Hugo, Emerson, Einstein, Lincoln, Carnegie, and Edison. Wallace D Wattles, whose 1910 book, *The Science of Getting Rich,* inspired Byrnes' book, adds Descartes to the list. Wattles also wrote *The Science of Being Well,* which is my favorite. In it, Wattles specifies that our attention must be on our healthy bodies which is the natural state. He advises us to think in a "certain way." Through thinking in that way, we may attract health and wealth and all good things. We must not give our attention to illness, disease, or physical complaints. Our bodies, he maintains, are capable of healing themselves. To what extent we might choose to accept this is, of course, a personal choice and balanced by the miracles of modern medicine. An over-reliance on those miracles may ignore the miracle of our own self-healing. However, one thing is sure: if we focus on good things, good things continue to happen accompanied by happiness. The opposite is also true. We are likely to get what we expect. Can there be a clearer choice? It is also clear that we need to be deliberate in our expectations. Abraham Hicks recommends that you divide the day into segments and state your expectations for that segment. Do not forget to include expectations, perhaps you formerly assumed, that you be healthy, safe, and protected. In this way, we can control our thoughts and be purposeful in our thinking. We may also call up positive energy and protection.

Before you leave for work in the mornings, perhaps following your prayers, you might communicate your requests and expectations to the cosmos, to the Creator, and to your inner being: I ask and expect safety and protection. I ask and expect direction and clear sailing. I ask and expect to be a blessing to others this day and to serve. I ask and expect the confidence and ability to do all that I need to do and to do it well. Perhaps you would choose to follow that with your expression of gratitude.

Chapter 13

The Power of Gratitude

I would maintain that thanks are the highest form of

thought, and that gratitude is happiness doubled by

wonder.

--G. K. Chesterton

GRATITUDE IS A practice that is vital to our spirits. I have mentioned it several times before, but now I'd like to send it to you as a *divine telegram*. It is indispensable to our soul's expansion and growth. I urge you to make yourself aware, on a constant basis, of the gifts and the benevolence of our universe. Take nothing for granted. Observe the multitude of presents the universe bestows on you. Louise Hay once suggested that when you get out of bed in the morning that you say "Thank" as you place your foot on the ground, and "You" as you place the other foot. When I read her words I was recovering from a broken foot. Believing that there are no coincidences, I took her words as an immediate divine telegram. I vowed to myself to never again get out of bed without consciously being thankful for each healthy foot. How many blessings do we overlook in a day? To be aware and conscious of each and every blessing would make anger or depression simply inconceivable. Resolve never again to walk through life blind to the grace of our God and the universal intelligence, however you understand it. In so doing, you will become a gift and an inspiration to those you love and care about. Keeping a gratitude journal is a good stress reliever. It restores perspective when we're dealing with problems and annoyances; it helps give clarity to life. Gratitude must be a daily practice. The universe loves our gratitude and rewards us with more to be grateful about. Conversely, when we are focused on what we don't have, we get more lack! When you are complaining to others about your aches and pains, you get more aches and pains. Abraham Hicks calls it The Law of Attraction. Others may call it The Secret. We attract what we think about. When you are in a constant state of gratitude, it is not possible to be miserable.

Commit yourself to developing your awareness of your blessings, and do not neglect the smallest ones! In the aggregate, they may be the most valuable. One idea for the daily expression of gratitude: I give thanks for all my many blessings, especially for those blessings that I don't even notice and for which I have not given thanks in the past. I give thanks for the people in my life and for the opportunities I have been given and will be given today. I am grateful for my very life and health. Next, you might intercede on behalf of others and of our planet. Many minds, many souls uniting in prayer and intercession are mighty to contemplate. A sense of gratitude truly nourishes the soul.

Showing gratitude is an essential part of our spiritual practice. It lightens our mood raises our awareness, and activates the brain's emotion center. It helps us to have a more complete perspective on our lives while enhancing our connectedness to others. We are indeed connected to the larger universe.

Chapter 14

Connections to Our Source and to One Another

A sick thought can devour the body's flesh more than

fever or consumption.

--Guy de Maupassant

THROUGH YOUR THOUGHTS you can influence, if not determine, your physical health. You can bring your goals from dreams to fruition. You can create or deepen your relationships. You can build a project, corporation, house, work of art, or fortune. It does require discipline. Visualize, then realize. Believe it; then conceive it. Recognize the powerful force of thoughts and then begin to use them constructively. Avoid using them destructively. For many of us, this necessitates a tidal wave of behavioral change. We have a tool at our disposal that can bring all of our hopes and dreams to fruition. How can we not use it?

There are elements in our current culture that do not positively contribute to spiritual growth. It is for each of us to determine what those are and to choose our response. The first response may be awareness or acknowledgement. A second response may be to strategize avoidance or change.

Our culture may have changed our thinking about many valuable things. Do we really encounter new ideas with open minds? Do we ever ridicule what we don't understand or don't agree with? Do we examine ideas or quickly accept or discard them? Are we willing to risk being wrong? Do we judge others and, if so, do we judge fairly? Do aspects of our culture keep us from learning and progressing? Do we rush through life? Do we enjoy our lives? Do we live life or observe it? This would be a great topic of discussion among friends and acquaintances, not in order to be right or impress our listeners, but in order to exchange ideas and gently challenge one another.

We need to also question our treatment of others. How do we acknowledge the presence of others that we pass or meet in the course of a day? I always feel uplifted when someone meets my eyes and exchanges smiles or greetings. Some people have a "me first" orientation, while others have an "after you" approach to life. Largely, we seem to attract those who think like us--the law of attraction at work.

In societies where older people garner greater respect as they age, people live longer. We all need to be needed and valued.

We are all connected, whether or not we acknowledge it. Not only are we connected with the family of man, we are also connected to our Source and the universe in ways that we are only beginning to comprehend. The famous American physicist, Albert Einstein, said, "Strange is our situation here upon Earth. Each of us comes for a short visit, not knowing why, yet sometimes seeming to a divine purpose. From the standpoint of daily life, however, there is one thing we do know: that we are here for the sake of others….with the countless unknown souls with whose fate we are connected by a bond of sympathy. Many times a day I realize how much my outer and inner life is built upon the labors of people, both living and dead, and how earnestly I must exert myself in order to give in return as much as I have received."

Search YouTube for the "Symphony of Science--We Are All Connected" featuring Carl Sagan, Bill Nye, Richard Feynman and other scientists. It truly is an experience for the senses and makes the point about our connectivity quite expressively.

Once you open yourself to the connectivity, it leads to awareness, followed by positive proof that we are indeed the family of man and connected to spirit and to the Source of all things. That brings awareness that things are just as they should be and that all is well.

Our bodies are indeed connected to the earth and that connection needs to be reestablished daily through a process known as *grounding*. The process of grounding helps us to relieve stress and anxiety and to steady our minds through the body's connection with the earth. If this sounds way out to you, first learn more about how the earth and its ions power energizes us and, second, try it. Experience it, not once, but in a cumulative fashion. While particularly important to people suffering from trauma or post-traumatic stress disorder, it is also necessary and desirable for all of us. It is a stabilizing force for our physical bodies and helps us not to be overwhelmed by our emotions. Being grounded helps us bring ourselves back to the present moment. But it also does much, much more.

If you love walking barefoot on the beach, you have already embraced grounding. It is said to be most beneficial barefoot in a lake or ocean or merely in the early morning dew.

Our ancestors were closely connected to the ground, largely through hunting, farming, and walking wherever they went and sleeping on the ground at night. Many of us, however, rarely touch the earth, instead walking laced up on pavement and riding in vehicles. Most of human knowledge and understanding of the value of being in touch with the earth is still in the future.

Chapter 15

Acceptance

Ask not that events should happen as you will, but let
your will be that events should happen as they do, and
you shall have peace.

--Epictetus

AS WE PROCEED through life dominated by our egos and attempting to control all aspects of living, and perhaps even trying to control those around us, there comes a time when we are confronted by the necessity of accepting something we do not want, did not ask for, and are unwilling to accept. After the initial frustration and anger, we are faced with making a choice: whether to continue to lash out against the inevitable or finally to adjust to our last resort acceptance. Acceptance is one of the huge life lessons that come to us all eventually. If it comes later in life, it is that much harder to learn.

The need for acceptance is generally learned when we're confronted with some challenge beyond human control. I learned it during the illness and subsequent death of my parents. Prior to that, I had felt some degree of control, imagined or real, over the majority of my experiences and situations. I fought the inevitable to the point of exhaustion or desperation, and then I had no choice but to accept. I was very much aware that I was learning a lesson I did not want to learn.

Acceptance is not the anathema that it may appear on the surface to be. Many of us have some degree of control issues that fill us with expectations about how things must be. Inflexible expectations set us up for disappointment and frustration. Life is fluid. Go with the flow, as they say, and you will spare yourself pain. Confucius advised us that the solution for many of life's problems is to "Adjust your expectations." Long ago I adopted that as my personal philosophy in life and I recommend it to anyone who will listen! The trick is to adjust those expectations prior to an event rather than after disappointment has occurred.

Inflexibility of will is a characteristic of ego. We do not control the universe and to assert through our willfulness and behavior that we do is swimming upstream. We are each a puzzle piece in the universe, and we must sometimes adapt in order to fit. We don't try to change the other pieces to adapt to us. At times, our physical presence in others' lives is about them! If you're held up in traffic, it may be that the timing is to enable you to have an influence on someone or to cross the path of someone who needs your intervention or influence. (Or it may even be to save your life in an accident that is about to occur.) Our very role and purpose is to serve, even when not by our own design. The universe uses us in many capacities even as it serves our needs. To complain about that use, to complain about delay or other matters beyond our control is fruitless. To refuse to accept is to refuse to serve.

Chapter 16

Energy

We cannot live only for ourselves. A thousand fibers connect us with our fellow men, and among those fibers, as sympathetic threads, our actions run as causes, and they come back to us as effects.

--Herman Melville

THROUGHOUT THE AGES, there has been an understanding or belief by human beings that we are connected to the cosmos by some energy related to our breathing. This energetic force has been called chi, ki or qi, prana, mana, kundalini, and countless other names. While I have the most limited comprehension of physics, it appears that scientists recognize that matter is a form of energy that vibrates at different frequencies. Energy is said to make up 98% of the universe and matter makes up the other 2%. Energies assume their forms based on their vibrational frequencies. Every atom vibrates at a frequency, and all matter is composed of atoms. What differentiates one object from another is its rate of vibration. Even emotions and thoughts have their own frequencies. Ancient Eastern healing techniques recognize that self-healing begins with vibrational energy. It is believed by many Eastern healers that over 95% of weakness and illness in the physical body is attributable to the emotions held or experienced by the individual. This is very persuasive to many of us that self-healing is largely a matter of guarding our thoughts and emotions and guiding our minds and consciousness in a positive way. Doctors trained in the West, specifically allopathic doctors, are truly brilliantly trained but do not receive training in diagnosing on the energetic level largely because it is not yet a value held by western physicians. By evaluating the physical body solely, they may not see what an analysis of the energetic body would reveal.

All life begins and ends with the breath. It is the breath that carries the Prana, or life force energy through our bodies. Our breath sustains our lives and must be understood and utilized.

If you hold your own two palms together but not touching, you will feel your own energy. We must understand our energy and come to understand our vibration. I picture it in this way: Our Creator, the Source of all good things and the Source of life, sends a vibrational energy out to all of us all of the time and, if we are open to it (not closed off through anger, blame, criticism, fear, and the like), that loving energy will flow through our bodies, raising our vibrational frequencies, energy, and creativity, enabling us to function at our highest potential. It is believed by many that the souls of the departed vibrate on a different frequency, inhibiting their and our ability to communicate. Some mediums claim to speed up their vibrations in order to communicate with the departed. Mediums tell us that the souls that communicate through them are concerned with the vibrational differences and how that interferes with their communication to us.

We should aspire to staying in spirit throughout each day, sending out that loving energy. Our ego has the potential to interfere with that flow and staunch our creativity and loving energy. Resist. Let the energy flow through you. That is your power. It will guide you in all things.

Chapter 17

Intention

Commitment is an act, not a word.

--Jean-Paul Sartre

WHAT IS IT that you want to accomplish in your life? State your intentions to yourself and commit to follow through with them. Rev yourself up daily. Find the most effective methods to energize yourself. Positive energy is the vehicle. When someone says "I'll try," that's no commitment. Do it or don't do it. But don't "try." That's an escape hatch. Intention is key. Write down your wildly improbable goal and then begin to achieve it. Keep your thoughts in check and revise them whenever necessary. Gradually, you will train your thoughts to formulate positive beliefs.

Often, when people get wonderful ideas, perhaps for a new business or endeavor of some sort, the mind jumps first to paying for it. The person may attempt to get a loan either from the bank or from family or friends. Some even begin to run up their credit card balance in an effort to subsidize their ideas. I don't believe that this is the place to start. On the contrary, great ideas begin in the universe and inspire our minds and hearts. Begin an initiative with prayer and meditation. Do both of these very consciously. Ask for guidance and means. Ask that doors may be opened. Ask for inspiration and initiative. Perhaps you may ask for a mentor or a partner. Ask that you may learn all you need to know. Accept divine inspiration and welcome it. And be grateful. Above all be grateful.

Intention implies that the individual puts his passion, resources, energy, thought, and ultimate commitment into the goal at hand. It is a marathon rather than a sprint. As many have found, discouragement is encountered at times along the way. The faint-hearted may give up or give in just around the corner from success. This is another one of the tests of the universe I think. The implication is that if you really want it nothing can stop you. And indeed it does appear to be darkest before the dawn.

Lacking intention, we often flounder and wander, dithering as we stray, seemingly without direction or purpose. But with the power of intention, all the forces of the universe appear to come together to throw wide the doors of opportunity. Next comes hard work, more discouragement perhaps, followed by more hard work. Then you ride that wave to shore!

Chapter 18

The End of This Life

I sent myself through the invisible, some letter of that afterlife to spell; and by and by my soul return to me, and answered, "I myself am Heav'n and Hell."

--Omar Khayyam

YOU WILL LIVE forever. Your soul will indeed live forever. And it has been living for ages. It is wise and wonderful. Your personality is not your soul but an earthly expression of it, often polluted by negative aspects of our culture, such as an obsession with money, youth, celebrity and force.

You are on this earth in order to accomplish some mission. You left the spirit world to come and, in time, you shall return to the spirit world and to your loved ones there. You need not fear the death of the body any more than the cicada fears the disposal of his shell. Once a body has been worn out with disease or with use, the body has ceased to be a proper vessel for the soul.

> *You mustn't be afraid of death*
> *You're a deathless soul*
> *You can't be kept in a dark grave*
> *You're filled with God's glow*

> --By Rumi

Our attitudes toward death and dying need some redefinition and perhaps change. For many, there is great fear and trepidation regarding the end of life. For some, the fear of death ruins the enjoyment of life. That is a terrible waste of beautiful living. To worry and agonize is a waste of life; there is no need for this. Certainly, no one wants to die young or leave their families or be left by their loved ones. Intellectually, we understand that death is another stage of life and we must accept it. It is not to be dreaded or feared. It is not the end of our being! Our personality and ego ceases as it is no longer needed for the next phase of existence but the source of our inner voice--the soul--goes on and on. We have soul goals to accomplish during our life, and doubtless we have additional soul goals in the next phase of spirit life.

The breeze at dawn has secrets to tell you.

Don't go back to sleep!

You must ask for what you really want.

Don't go back to sleep!

People are going back and forth across the doorsill

where the two worlds touch,

The door is round and open

Don't go back to sleep!

--By Rumi

Chapter 19

Knowing the Truth From Within

*The intuitive mind is a sacred gift and the rational
mind is a faithful servant. We have created a society
that honors the servant and has forgotten the gift.*

--Albert Einstein

WHEN I DISCOVERED the work of David R.
Hawkins, M.D., Ph.D., my perception of the world changed.
This is no small statement to make. An idealist by nature,
I had become disillusioned and skeptical. There seemed to
me to be an absence of truth, validity, and spirit everywhere
I looked. I became disenfranchised regarding politics,
government, and the global economic market. I looked

within myself and saw the same duplicity and failure to admit the truth even to myself. I became aware that what we tell ourselves, the beliefs and the excuses we make harm ourselves, minds, and bodies. I felt, however, that it was very difficult to arrive at the truth. The truth is hidden behind layers of subterfuge. I suspect that this is pervasive around the globe. If so, I am convinced that we have to "get real." If people cannot recognize the truth when they hear it, they are making decisions and coming to conclusions erroneously. They are cheated. It effects how they conduct themselves towards others; they may cheat others as well. It is as if we are all blind to the truth. We have very little experience hearing truth, and we cannot recognize it. We may not know the truth. I believe that is why I had such an emotional reaction to hearing the government official own up to the truth. It was a new experience!

We must make dramatic global changes in the way we conduct ourselves and relate to one another. We certainly have access to abundant information about how to make societal changes, protect our Mother Earth, bring about peace, stamp out starvation, and the like. While we lack will, compassion, determination and direction, the primary lack is consciousness. We must unite our individual consciousness with that of others. Direction will emerge and our will and determination will build. Einstein once said that he didn't know how World War III would be fought, but that World War IV would be fought with sticks and stones. While our earthly problems are many, our knowledge and resources far exceed them when we combine forces, forces of consciousness. All of this is a part of getting real! Politicians will not accomplish this. Leadership will come from among the spiritual students of metaphysics. One is Dr. David Hawkins.

David Hawkins' book *Power Versus Force, The Hidden Determinants of Human Behavior*, explains that by using our own muscles, our bodies can reveal truth and falsehood and determine value, or lack of value, using kinesiological testing. We hold that power within our own bodies! Our own bodies know the truth.

The body knows that is good for it (example: organic fruit) and, through muscle testing, is able to convey that to us. In the presence of artificial sweetener, the muscle goes weak. The body also knows truth. When people are muscle tested about the veracity of statements they are hearing from a speaker, the results are startling. Hawkins describes a "database of consciousness" or shared knowledge that can determine healthy or unhealthy, true or false. Perhaps our spirits are combining with the universal consciousness to convey truth to us. The implications are staggering! Imagine the application to courts of law, to the political process, the health establishment, and the economic system, as well as to our individual lives.

Hawkins also analyzed the levels of human consciousness and calibrated a scale of the truth of ideas, beliefs, and philosophies that ranges from 1 to 1,000. His work is so detailed and scientific that it does not bear summarizing and must be read firsthand. The kinesiological testing also requires careful attention to detail. He has produced a chart that every person should become acquainted. Hawkins' own astounding experiences have brought him closer to the enlightenment he describes. His personal experiences illustrate energetic powers of which I believe many or all are capable if only we would perceive and harness them. Hawkins would possibly correct that statement to read that those who calibrate above the level of 200 would be able to perceive and harness energetic power. Through his studies he has indicated that Buddha, Jesus Christ, and Mohammed, among very few others, calibrated at 1,000. Hawkins states also that, "It's only the illusion of individuality that is the origin of all suffering—when one realizes that one is the universe, complete and at one with all that is, forever without end, then no further suffering is possible." Simply stated, we are all connected. Each of our actions has ramifications on others. And the most profound effect we have on one another is to love them, to send out love no matter what we get back. We are all a work in progress. And within each of us is a spark of the God Material, or the Divine Presence, or the Source. Hawkins states that "All pain and suffering arises solely from the ego and not from God." As a physician, he tried to convey this belief to his patients, and he asked them not to blame God for what their egos had done to them. As long as we displace responsibility for our actions and beliefs to others, even to God, we lose the power to change. We begin living with kindness and sending love and energy out into the world to spread to others.

Hawkins maintains that kinesiology is the connector between the physical world, the mind, and the spirit. He used it to test every "substance, thought, and concept I could think of." Through his work, he made a startling discovery that, although everyone tested went weak from negative stimuli (fluorescent lights, pesticides, etc.), people who were spiritual students of consciousness weren't as affected because they didn't see themselves at the mercy of the world, but were more affected by what they believed. As we move closer to enlightenment huge changes occur and we gain more protection. We travel this road to enlightenment, via consciousness. Consciousness is achieved largely through meditation.

In the meditative state, we are in contact with the Divine, to a greater or lesser degree. As students of consciousness, we increase that degree more and more. Fear is replaced by joy and peace. Our awareness begins to illuminate ourselves and our place in the cosmos. We become more patient and kind toward ourselves and others. As the ego releases thoughts, desires, and awareness of self, a greater awareness of our mission comes into increased focus. Hawkins believed that our suffering and our pain were caused by our egos; it does not come from God. There is no death. The body becomes superfluous. Learning from the masters tells me that as we move into higher consciousness, we relinquish the existence of ego and self as the main determinant and eventually join the universal consciousness.

Chapter 20

Spiritual Laws of the Universe

Place yourself in the middle of the stream of power and wisdom which animates all whom it floats, and you are without effort impelled to truth, to right, and a perfect contentment.

--Ralph Waldo Emerson

THERE ARE SPIRITUAL laws in the universe. Through thought, meditation, and experience, these become illuminated. If you are working within the laws, you eventually receive a good outcome. If you transgress the laws, you suffer in order to learn a better way. However, if you displace responsibility for your suffering onto others, make excuses, or otherwise do not accept responsibility for your choices, you fail to learn lessons and you fail or delay the evolution into the enlightened being you were meant to be. Perhaps the first law of the universe that I learned through experience was to think in positive terms, to expect good things to happen, to expect to be successful at what I attempted, and to expect a good outcome. If my thinking became negative, my outcome also became negative. As I began to see this pattern emerge, I experienced an "aha!" moment. When negative thoughts enter my mind, I immediately cast them out and replace them with thoughts of how I want things to be. We could call this the law of free will. I am largely responsible for my experiences and for how I explain those experiences to myself. If I blame someone else, or view God as orchestrating all the moves, I will not be exercising free will. If I make poor choices that hurt or fail to help others, I am also using my free will and there will be repercussions. One likely repercussion is that I will be presented with a similar scenario repeatedly until

I get it right. The universe tries to teach me and steps up the lessons if I fail to learn them.

One of the people I love most on earth chooses to rush through life. He's always in a hurry. He walks fast, drives fast, frequently runs late and tries to compensate for it. One autumn day we were driving to a nearby town to take some important papers to a friend. I commented on the beauty of the leaves. He answered that we didn't have time to look around because we needed to deliver these papers! I believe he was unaware of the sacrifice he was making. Every moment spent rushing is a moment of life not fully enjoyed. If you add up all of those moments, you risk missing a substantial portion of your life. My chief concern about his habit of rushing is that the universe keeps stepping up his lessons and the risk continues to increase until he finally learns the life lesson to stop and smell the roses, to notice and appreciate the world as he walks through each day. It seems as though we learn more quickly from pain than we do from other experiences. The universe offers us the opportunity to learn from our experiences and to coexist peacefully with the spiritual law of wisdom.

There are likely many other spiritual laws as well. It is part of our journey and life experience to discover them. Here are some that I have stumbled upon in my search, many through study and some through personal experience.

One of my favorite laws is the law of grace. It is a merciful law that mitigates our "just desserts" based on our showing mercy, kindness, and understanding to those around us. It is often known as Karma, although I believe that Karma entails much more. Grace is the benevolent giving and receiving of calm guidance and many second chances followed by undeserved and perhaps unwarranted gifts of forgiveness and latitude in our life learning. We give grace to others as well as receive it through unconditional love. Grace is not necessarily deserved; often it is not. Most of us would admit that often we have received wonderful gifts that were undeserved. Each time we act mercifully to others, as we open our hearts with love and compassion, we grant grace to others. We subsequently receive grace, perhaps through a powerful insight, a life-changing event, a release from fear or worry, an act of kindness by another, or even a physical healing. Divine qualities such as caring, compassion, assistance, empathy, love, and mercy attract grace into our own lives.

The law of gratitude is a powerful law indeed. The more assistance you bestow on others in their walk through this life, the more you assist yourself. Your load is lightened; your mission becomes clearer; your spirit is pleased and you feel that pleasantness inside you. The universe loves gratitude and gives you the opportunity to receive even more for which to be grateful. Become aware that those things you formerly called problems are life lessons. Be thankful for them. They help you grow. When my marriage was failing over 30 years ago, through marriage counseling I was led to a career in counseling. It was not a career that I had considered. But when I experienced counseling, I knew that I had to help provide that experience to others.

It amazes me now that I did not make that connection for several years afterward. Then I was grateful. I was also a recipient of grace. The gratitude journal is my tool for disciplining myself to recognize my blessings and be thankful for them. I highly recommend it to anyone who will listen. Go through your day gathering the blessings for which you will be grateful. Celebrate life. Live in a state of joy.

The law of resistance states that if you resist something you are drawing that experience to yourself. It happens throughout our lives, and many educators recognize the value and often utilize it in the training of young professionals in a variety of fields. During my counseling internship some years ago, I was working in a therapy clinic of a hospital. I was supervised by several outstanding and experienced therapists. Primarily, I was working with individuals who had behavior related difficulties, as well as people with mental illnesses. I was assigned a patient for counseling who was preparing to undergo sex change surgery. I asked my supervisor to rescind that assignment because I felt I had little to offer the patient. I had minimal understanding of his needs and didn't feel capable of helping him. Naturally, and in accordance with spiritual law, I was told that I would indeed be his therapist. Feeling somewhat overwhelmed, I began to wonder what a person preparing to become a woman might need to know or experience. Most of my later counseling career was spent in educational settings but I often had the chance to reflect on that experience and to recognize that by resisting something, I was attracting it to me.

Today, when I find myself resisting someone who is stubborn, for instance, I ask myself to become aware of my own stubborn quality. When I tend to resist people who I see as being ego filled, I look for the egocentrism within me. When I am lied to and feel anger and resistance, I ask myself in what ways am I not being truthful with myself and others. That which you dislike about yourself, you will dislike in others as well. Resistance to something indicates your fear of that thing.

I particularly wish that the United States government would understand this natural law of attraction and never again declare a war on poverty (we now have greater poverty) or a war on drugs (drugs are rampant in our society). With the problems we are now experiencing in our schools, it is as if the US government had declared a war on education!

The law of attraction states that you will attract that which you focus your mind and energy on. "Where your attention goes, your energy flows." Structure your thinking so that you attract the things you want. You want safety, good health, kindness, cooperation from others, good fortune, support, and success. Give thought to those things and how they might be attained. Do not dwell on illness, loss, and misfortune. Use your energy positively. You can attract that which you do not want if you put your energy into driving it away. Instead, think as though that which you want to attract is already present in your life. Behave as though it is. Feel and express the gratitude of having it in your life. Feel the joy and jubilation. Celebrate it!

The law of fellowship states that there is magnification of achieved purpose when two or more people gather together for that purpose. The Bible states this law that "when two or more are gathered in His name" the message is amplified as is the reception of the message. Most world religions recognize this law. There is currently a trend toward worldwide meditations to promote peace and end hunger. I strongly believe in the efficacy of these efforts and I participate in them.

No doubt you are intimately familiar with the law of forgiveness. Earlier, we talked about the healing quality of forgiveness. Both the forgiver and the one forgiven experience the healing. Forgiving is an act of love, compensated by grace, often in the form of emotional or physical healing. Healing occurs due to the high frequency vibration of love overcoming the low vibrations of anger, fear, resentment, and other forms of pain. Forgive and open yourself to grace.

Perhaps the sister of grace is the law of faith. Faith could be described as intent listening to one's inner voice, your personal guidance and intuition, and following that voice with confidence. Faith gives birth to miracles while driving out fear.

Like grace, faith is a high-frequency quality that brings about those miracles. When we are in the presence of someone of great faith, we feel it. The faithful exude self-confidence and we feel it in their presence. We feel it in ourselves as well. Faith is powerful and it makes us powerful.

The spiritual law of blessings is invoked when you direct divine energy towards the person you are blessing. Blessing others stirs up positive energy that blesses that person as well are yourself and I believe even others on the periphery. I visualize the blessing as circular energy that pervades even bystanders! A physician friend of mine told me that on his long railroad ride to work each morning, he systematically blesses each patient he will work with and each medical person who will assist him or attend to the patient. Then he begins to bless each person in each row on the train. He is conferring divine energy on each person he blesses and, through grace, he is blessed. I like to visualize those blessings as wafting gently through the air toward their intended recipients and dripping blessings on the shoulders of those walking below!

Give out abundant blessings! Bless the business that serves you well. Bless the homeless people you see on the corner, the children you see playing in a school yard, the people in the ambulance speeding by, the inhabitants of hospitals, schools, and nursing homes that you pass by. Bless whole groups of people: the hungry, the ill, the down-trodden, those serving the hungry, ill and down-trodden. Bless those enforcing the law and even those breaking the law. Bless all babies born today. Bless the souls of all those that died today and bless their families who mourn them. Bless each and every student in all schools around the globe. Bless their teachers and their parents. Bless your plants and watch them grow. Bless your animals and wildlife everywhere. Invite divine energy unto yourself and to others. Become a blessing.

Perhaps the law I have struggled most with is the law of allowing. This law requires us to experience the freedom of allowing circumstances to be what they are and people to be who they are. While I have recognized control issues in my husband and others, it was far more difficult to recognize my own control issues. And the recognition of those issues pales in difficulty to the law of allowing things to take their course without my personal intervention! Perhaps you understand this on a personal level yourself. However, there is great liberation in eventually comprehending that you are not responsible for the world and those living in it. I urge you not to interfere in the life lessons of others unless you see critical danger ahead.

The law of healing states that there is healing energy within us. Divine power, the power of our Source, our God, activates the healing energy within us and we are able to heal ourselves, or the energy can pass through us to heal others. With intent, we possess the power to send healing energy into the past, present, or future. The accelerator for the healing energy is meditation. My most recently received divine telegram came shortly before I awoke. I heard one phrase: Your DNA needs meditation. I am trying to embrace that information and utilize it. I believe that it enables healing even at the cellular level. Like you, I am on the path to learning these skills. I am utilizing the law of faith to manifest self-healing.

There may be a myriad of other spiritual laws as well. They are ours to discover, practice, and share. I believe that we must share what we learn with others. We then combine our knowledge, collaborate in a myriad of ways and, consequently, extend the knowledge of mankind.

Chapter 21

Living in Spirit

Cherish your visions and your dreams, as they are the children of your soul, the blueprints of your ultimate achievements.

--Napoleon Hill

I URGE YOU to set aside the next hour to a commitment to live in spirit. Control your thoughts and insure that they are pure, loving and judgment free. Begin by meditating and opening yourself up to the universe, your Source, your inner voice, your spirit guide, perhaps even your ancestors. Ask for inspiration and insight.

Embrace silence and learn to love it. Learn also to hear your thoughts and to be aware of your feelings and reactions to what you see, hear, and experience. Learn to listen, not just with your ears but with your soul. Ask your body if there is anything wrong within your body. "Please tell me anything I need to know." Then listen. Listen and feel. If your attention is drawn to a particular area of your body, ask follow-up questions. Just realize that answers may not come immediately and swiftly. They may come on the universe's time, on your spirit's time, and in unexpected ways. They may be figurative rather than literal. You have no control over how they are sent or received. Whenever or however they come, you've just received delivery of a divine telegram. Be grateful; more are coming. The lines of communication between you and your spirit are now opening.

You will become more and more familiar with how the universe and your own spirit communicate. My experience has been that the communications surprise or even shock me and sometimes seem as though the sender has a sense of humor!

When one of my daughters was expecting a baby, I asked the universe, very early in her pregnancy, to let me see her baby. I repeated this request several times before I fell asleep. About four or four-thirty that morning, I awoke with a clear understanding that I had just seen my soon-to-be granddaughter. But rather than seeing her as a baby, I saw her as a grown woman, at an age that I would be unlikely to get to see her during my lifetime. Seeing her as an adult was a surprise to me. It was not at all what I had expected! But what shocked me was the look in her eyes as her eyes met mine. It was a knowing. We truly knew each other and recognized each other. It was a look of knowing and love. Seeing that vision of her let me know that she will be a capable woman who will accomplish a great deal in this world. I saw her and knew her. That is all I can say because that is all that I currently understand. I hope to put this divine telegram into better context as life goes on.

About a year ago, a neighbor and dear friend who'll I'll call "Mike" became very ill. We all knew, and he knew, that it was just a matter of time before he died. We talked about his death and he told me some of his regrets, and we tried to come to terms with the inevitable. One night, again very early in the morning just before awakening, I clearly saw in my mind's eye, as though I was standing in my driveway, a gigantic wildly flowered white funeral wreath on a gigantic stand in his former driveway (as he had recently moved two miles away), facing not the road but facing me. It was not a traditional funeral wreath by any means. It was not even a wreath. It was a beautiful, white overgrown profusion of flowers. I immediately, though asleep, knew its meaning. I sat up and awakened my poor husband, who is quite accustomed to my early morning "visions", for lack of a better word. I said, "Mike just died." He replied that we'd probably hear sometime in the day and to try to go back to sleep. (As if that's possible!) As the day wore on we heard nothing from his wife. I couldn't understand it. My husband called several times during the day to ask if I'd heard from Janice. I had not. I felt confused because on the rare occasions when I have these visions, they had thus far been trustworthy. I was frankly amazed. Shortly before nine that night Janice did call and confirmed that Mike had passed early in the morning.

One night about six months ago we went out to a Mexican Restaurant in town. As I got up to go to the restroom, I waved at a friend Bob and his wife. As I entered the restroom I had a vision of Bob looking emaciated. When I returned to my table, Bob and his wife were gone. My husband said they had stopped by the table to say hello. I asked if Bob looked ill or as if he had lost a great deal of weight. My husband said that, on the contrary, he looked as if he had gained weight. I didn't know what to make of that and still do not, although I've not seen him in three months or more. This was my first experience of having a sense of dread brought on my one of my so-called visions.

Today, on the very day I am writing this, I had my first semi-vision while awake. I looked out a window as I passed by and thought I saw another neighbor, Dick, walking down my driveway. I went to my front door but no Dick. That seemed strange. A couple of hours later, the doorbell rang and there stood Dick, holding a loaf of freshly baked bread, still hot!

I'm not sure why I'm writing about these experiences, perhaps to come to an eventual understanding and acceptance that I'm having these visions and perhaps to understand why.

Each time I have a vision, I take notes and describe the details and memories that I recall. I've had a few others as well, though not many. What I recall most vividly about each is my emotions during that vision. I'm not sure why I have visions now when I did not for my first 50-plus years. My only explanation is that my mind has grown slightly more open and I have had the time to think, meditate, learn, and now to write.

In this way, I believe that the soul and aspects of the universe communicate with me. I feel I am in the infant stage of what is possible. So much learning is ahead. More questions are raised regarding my friend Bob: Why would I have seen this vision? Is it valid? What am I to do; what steps should I take? I see myself as being a student of the spiritual universe. I have so much to learn. At this point I have chosen to continue to learn and to try to inspire others to join me in the spiritual school. Here, I've saved a seat for you!

If you rule out the possibility of second sight, you have simultaneously denied yourself the chance to possess that ability. The western world has largely done this. Our minds are more powerful than we know and, by our beliefs we enable or disable our abilities. During the first 50 or more years of my life, my mind was largely closed to such possibilities as second sight or precognition. But then I began to have experiences that I could not deny and that I sought to explain. I believe that I had my first experience in order to avoid serious illness. Gradually, I became open to possibilities. Now I embrace my urges, insights, and visions. I urge you to consider doing the same. Gradually I make sense of them or my life seems to integrate them in a way I eventually came to understand.

Chapter 22

Energetic Beings

If you want to find the secrets of the universe, think in
terms of energy, frequency and vibration.

--Nicola Tesla

IF YOU HAVE a better knowledge of physics than I do, perhaps you will also have a superior understanding of energy. Most of us know that our bodies are composed of energy rather than solid matter, despite how it may appear. Even the refrigerator and couch are composed of energy. Therefore, perhaps it stands to reason that our own energy, chi, or qi, can be a healing source for our bodies, combined with our intent, personal belief, and commitment to healing. If you've always looked outside your body for solutions to the body's complaints, perhaps this is a paradigm shift for you. If, however, you break your leg, I am not suggesting that you meditate yourself to wholeness again! There are real and necessary reasons to consult allopathic physicians but there are also many instances when we can heal ourselves and other instances when homeopathic physicians can help us heal. Homeopathic solutions combined with allopathic medical care may be the most powerful combination when one is seriously ill. Perhaps when mankind possesses a full and complete understanding of energy and how to use it for healing, and when homeopathic and allopathic medicine both become part of medical school curriculum, we can also then prevent disease. Does it shock your senses to realize that we could move from a medical culture of treating disease to that of preventing disease? As a culture, it is our general habit to look outside ourselves for information and for solutions. We are raised and educated to think in this way. In so doing, however, we neglect our very best source: the soul within. Our souls have existed forever and their wisdom can and must be our guiding lights. First, we have to open our minds to the possibilities, then be quiet and listen. The soul will provide the answers and the guidance. Many among us, however, do not get past the first hurdle, to open our minds. There are astounding values to be shared among cultures when we are open to it. However, if we allow past limited understanding to dictate the capacity of our learning in the present, we remain stunted. While it is much easier and more comfortable to resist change, we cannot afford the cost. Deep down you know, and you are completely aware, even if you are resistant, that change is inevitable.

Embrace the inevitable. Learning and growing are synonymous. We are indeed energetic beings.

Everything has energy. Everything is composed of energy, including our own bodies. The lesson for humanity is to learn to embrace and nurture energy and to use it to our best effect. Our life force energy is known as chi or qi in many cultures. Using our chi to help us heal is perhaps most valuable. However, if you are unaware of chi, or if you choose to reject the idea of chi, then you also choose not to utilize it.

And it is a gift from our Source, our God, and our universe. There are many ways to use chi most effectively: reiki, chakra balancing, reflexology, grounding or earthing, acupuncture, acupressure, qi gong, yoga, tapping, and more. Despite what your "common sense" (i.e., habitual knowledge gained in the past dictated by experiences subsequent to that time only) may tell you, commit yourself to experiencing some of these energetic healing sources for yourself. Postpone judgment until you have firsthand knowledge. In my own practicing of qi gong, I found that I had to try it several times before I could feel my own energy. Had I given up too soon, I might have made an unfortunate preliminary judgment that qi gong wouldn't work for me. As my senses sharpened and my mind cleared,

I was able to feel my own energy. It was then unbelievable to me that I had been unable to feel it before. Similarly, I spent several years attempting to see auras around my body and around other people. Auras are the physical representation of the body's energy. One day I finally saw the aura around my hand. I had probably attempted to see it hundreds, perhaps thousands of times previously. Again, had I not persevered, I would never have seen my aura and never come to believe or understand. As it is, it is now a valuable tool in my personal arsenal of healing and tuning techniques. And yet, I recognize that I am a rookie in the observation and use of the auric field. Our preconceived ideas can work to our detriment so we must be aware of them and put them aside in order to learn and adjust to new events and circumstances.

One of the least understood concepts in the west regarding maintaining good health is our energy circuits or chakras. Western allopathic medicine, unlike allopathic physicians in the eastern and far eastern cultures, tend to hesitate or even disregard use of such enhancing therapies as art, music, dance. and movement, massage, nutrition and energetic balancing, while, if these therapies and approaches were utilized, it would only enhance healing after surgery or other treatment.

As a culture, we must embrace energetic healing as a complement to current medical practices. Many people have never tried harnessing their chi or energy for healing. They may not understand that our life-force energies must be properly conserved and directed toward healing when needed. The way to understanding is through an open mind and actually experimenting with your own chi. I first did this using the chi from the palms of my hands. I had to feel it to believe it. This did not happen the first several times. When I finally did feel it, I was amazed that I could have missed it earlier. As with seeing auras, you must soften your gaze and look peripherally rather than staring directing at your hand. With feeling your chi, you must feel with your whole body and not just with your fingertips. An example of this is when someone walks into a room without your noticing, but then you feel them. Your whole body alerted you. Your fingers touched nothing at all. After I was able to feel my chi--my life-force energy--I began to pass it back and forth, palm to palm as I might do with clay. I rolled it, packed it, and rolled it some more, and then used it, according to the tenets of Qi Gong, to heal my bruised knees from an earlier fall. I would take the "ball" of chi, and apply it to my knee, then pull it (and the injury) back out of the knee. I would do this many times while breathing in unison with my movements. I usually practiced the healing a couple of times a day, for 10 to 15 minutes each time. I concentrated without distraction during those sessions, while visualizing the healing. As I felt the heat and healing in my knees, I knew this was something valuable that deserved my further attention. This led me to the study of energetic healing and the functions of chakras. Once I understood the individual roles of each of the major chakras and the overall role of the organs they influenced or even controlled, I was flabbergasted at the ways some of my thoughts and behaviors had worked against my goal of excellent health. I found it astounding, for instance, that the pancreas, which is located in the third chakra, could be negatively affected or drained by my judgmental thoughts about others! How could this be? When I made harsh judgments, I actually lost energy from the third chakra, the solar plexus, which depleted the pancreas from accomplishing its mission to convert the food we eat into fuel for the use of our body's cells, to thus aiding in digestion and regulating the body's blood sugar. How then could I protect my pancreas? I knew the first step. I must do the hardest thing of all, change my thinking and my subsequent behaviors. Louise Hay, Carolyn Myss, and Barbara Ann Brennan are excellent mentors for this. Through their books and videos, I came to understand what I must do, why I must do it, and exactly how to proceed. I built on that and gradually came to know that although I could not control all aspects of my health, I could heavily influence it and my healing. I considered this to be vital information and I'm anxious to share it with you as well. It is worthy of pursuit. I do not pretend to know all of the factors that bring about illness in our bodies, but I do know some and I will do whatever is in my power to safeguard my health, and my overwhelming desire is to urge you to do likewise, despite how "out there" some of this information may appear to be.

There are many forms of energetic healing, including, but not limited to qigong, reflexology, reiki, massage, EFT. Certainly, energetic healing deserves much more investigation, hopefully followed by utilization. This information certainly gave me the impetus I needed to change my thoughts and behaviors.

Chapter 23

Living in Concert with Others

The energy of the mind is the essence of life.

--Aristotle

AS OUR CONSCIOUSNESS develops, I believe that the universe escalates attempts to lead us, guide us and enlighten us. The pragmatic person with the completely grounded thinking patterns might not be open to reception of many divine telegrams. Whether it is our spirit guides, angels, ancestors, or unknown entities, there are incoming messages if only we are open to receiving them. Coincidences and synchronicity attract our attention so that we can be listening and observing and appreciating divine telegrams as they are delivered. I have been astounded during the last few years at the ways the universe has focused my attention on incoming messages. When my attention has been focused on the messages, I must then perceive them in a way I can benefit. Over the past almost two years, I experienced a broken foot (without engaging in any particular act which brought about the break, as far as I know), then months later tripped and fell onto my knees (bringing about very sore and bruised knees but no real injury), and third, some months after that, I became annoyed by a disturbing feeling in one leg (sometimes called the "jimmy leg") that really bothered me as I tried to fall asleep at night. I saw these three experiences as a possible message to me. It was the coincidence and synchronized aspect of the three experiences that got my attention. I am currently in the process of analyzing them and attempting to decipher them. Initially my reaction was to be afraid to walk far from home or to only wear particularly supportive shoes. In other words, one of fear. I then began to change my thinking. Because I seek to find good in the universe and think that we live in a beautiful world, I searched for a positive interpretation of the message. I began to analyze my attitude toward my own aging, stepping out of my comfort zone and taking on more challenges. I began to interpret the message as one meant to urge me to step out there into life with more boldness. I began to think that I had been too passive in some aspects of my life choices, and that I was being urged to realize that I was crippling myself by seeking the path of least resistance. Once I began interpreting the message in an instructive and positive way, I abandoned my fear of walking, regained confidence and began to challenge myself, first in small ways and gradually in larger ones. So while it is still in progress, my behavior is changing in a positive way as a result of the three "coincidental" divine messages which I ultimately determined was one big alert from the universe. I am learning to take more dramatic steps to improve my life.

In the above example, while I was reacting to the events in my life with fear (fear of walking far from home, fear of wearing sandals, etc.), I did not receive the intended message. I think the universe sends positive messages. That has always been my experience. As I observe how our society behaves, I notice that when we are experiencing negative emotions, we are ineffective at accomplishing what we hope to accomplish. The "war on poverty" and the "war on drugs" were failures. Behavior that is fear based, defensive or offensive, goes against the intentions of the universe. Looking for insult or injury may cause you to find it, whether or not it is present. Rather, let us look for meaning in our dreams and our experiences. Let us examine our incoming messages for meaning.

Your thoughts about others influence, and may even dictate, the response of the universe to you. For example, if you harshly judge a person for his or her negative behavior and you fail to understand or find any reason in your heart why the person behaved the way he did, then you are simultaneously closing off the flow of "well-being," for lack of a better word, that flows from the universe to each of us. We must be sending out that same flow of well-being in order to be receiving it. That flow of well-being is so pervasive that it influences or even determines your spiritual blessings at any given time. Do not expect the flow of well-being while you are sending out a flow of judgment or condemnation. The negative feelings and thoughts you emit hurt your very own body and, in time, may cause disease. I first learned of this from Louise Hay in her life-changing book, *You Can Heal Your Life*. This should be required reading for all human beings! After reading that book, one should read *All is Well*, by Louise Hay and Mona Lisa Shultz M.D., Ph.D., which goes into tremendous detail about how our thoughts, beliefs, and attitudes bring about very specific diseases. Ideally, we would read these books as we emerge from the cradle, and avoid causing illness to our bodies. But, whatever your current age, these books are a must-read!

Our spirits and our physical bodies are very intertwined with those of others throughout the universe. I believe that the very thoughts of our ancestors are out there in the universe joining together with our own. Their souls continue to thrive and actively do the soul work of the spirit world, whatever that might be. Your soul will live forever. Accept that, and everything else falls into place. You lose your fear of death. You know that you will be reunited with those you have loved and lost. You know that their love for you continues and even multiplies! You know that they are safe and sound on a different spiritual plane. You understand your importance in the universe. You feel a connection to others in the universe, both living and "dead." In no way are they really dead, I believe, but merely functioning on a different energetic frequency, without the human ego or the temporary physical body, to distract, interrupt or derail their spiritual roles. We join together with those who have already lived a physical life on this planet, or perhaps elsewhere, if there are other "elsewheres"! Our human brains are probably incapable of comprehending the vastness of the universe. Yet we are interdependent in very real ways. Our thoughts, actions and feelings are very influential on the universe. I think we clearly understand that influence in our own towns or communities, but we may not yet accept that it is a truth that applies to the spiritual universe as well. If you are not yet ready to accept it, I hope you will at least be open to the possibility and await the proof in your own life. It will come, either through experience or through a divine telegram! Your work is to decipher it and utilize it in your life.

The world is changing very quickly. Globalization and access to amazing technology has meant that we can communicate with others who may be very far away or physically inaccessible. We can learn from them, exchange ideas, give and receive aid and assistance, exchange feelings of love, respect, and brotherhood and truly extend and optimize the human experience. Or we may choose to hold on to our preconceived notions about ourselves, our God and the universe, to judge others as inferior to ourselves, to exercise our power over those who do not believe as we do, and assault their way of living through attacks and warfare. The choice is ours. If we insulate ourselves and limit ourselves to our own personal concerns, we do not add our contributions to the universal consciousness. We short-change the universe out of what we have to offer. Thus we betray the earth, our island home.

How do you begin to open yourself up, I hope you are asking. My reply would be two-fold: meditation and education. Read, study, and learn from spiritual teachers. I have mentioned many of them in this book. You could start anywhere you like but I would suggest that you start with an understanding of how your thoughts influence the health of your very own physical body. That was my starting place and it has made all the difference. Through meditation, you will receive direction and you will open your mind. Meditation is absolutely crucial to the process, so please do not skip that step or tell yourself that you cannot master it. You will begin or continue the process of spiritual growth. Then join together with others to meditate. Create the stream of consciousness through which good will and inspiration flows. Then ride that stream throughout this life and into the next.

Bibliography

Brennan, B. A. (1987). *Hands of Light: A Guide to Healing Through the Human Energy Field.* New York: Bantam Books.

Byrne, R. (2006). *The Secret.* New York: Atria Books.

Byrne, R. (2012). *The Magic.* New York: Atria Books.

Davies, B. M. (2000). *The 7 Healing Chakras.* Berkeley: Ulysses Press.

Day, L. (1997). *Practical Institution for Success.* New York: HarperCollins Publishers, Inc.

Dyer, W. W. (2006). *Inspiration - Your Ultimate Calling.* Carlsbad: Hay House, Inc.

Dyer, W. W. (2009). *Excuses Be Gone!* Carlsbad: Hay House, Inc.

Dyer, W. W. (2012). *Wishes Fulfilled - Mastering the Art of Manifesting.* Carlsbad: Hay House, Inc.

Hawkins, D. R. (1995). *Power Vs. Force.* Carlsbad: Hay House, Inc.

Hay, L. L. (1999). *You Can Heal Your Life.* Carlsbad: Hay House, Inc.

Hay, L. L. (2013). *All is Well.* Carlsbad: Hay House, Inc.

Hill, N. (1937). *Think and Grow Rich: Revised and Updated for the 21st Century.* Chicago: Combined Registry Office.

Motz, J. (1998). *Hands of Life.* New York: Bantam Books.

Myss, C. (2001). *Invisible Acts of Power.* New York: Free Press.

Rankin, L. M. (2013). *Mind Over Medicine.* Carlsbad: Hay House, Inc.

Roth, R. P. (1997). *The Healing Path of Prayer.* New York: Three Rivers Press.

Sharma, R. S. (1997). *The Monk Who Sold His Ferrari.* New York: HarperOne.

Wattles, W. D. (2002). *The Wallace D. Wattles Collection of Self Improvement Books.* Tucson: Iceni Books.